Building Basic Skills in Writing

Book 1

Contemporary Books, Inc.
Chicago

Library of Congress Cataloging in Publication Data
Main entry under title:

Building basic skills in writing.

   1. English language—Grammar—1950–
2. Basic education.   I. Contemporary Books, inc.
PE1112.B74   808′.042   81-802
ISBN 0-8092-5880-3 (pbk.)   AACR2

Published by Contemporary Books, Inc.
180 North Michigan Avenue, Chicago, Illinois 60601
Manufactured in the United States of America
Library of Congress Catalog Card Number: 81-802
International Standard Book Number: 0-8092-5880-3

Published simultaneously in Canada by
Beaverbooks, Ltd.
150 Lesmill Road
Don Mills, Ontario M3B 2T5
Canada

ACKNOWLEDGMENTS

The thoughtful efforts of a great many people went into the preparation of Contemporary Books' *Building Basic Skills* series. We gratefully acknowledge their contributions and continued involvement in Adult Education.

Adult Education Division

Lillian J. Fleming, Editorial Director
Barbara Drazin, Editor
Wendy Harris, Marketing Services Coordinator

Production Department

Deborah Eisel, Production Editor

Reading and Readability Editors

Jane L. Evanson
Helen B. Ward
Norma Libman

Deborah Nathan
Jane Friedland
Donna Wynbrandt

Authors and Contributors

Writing: Rob Sax

Social Studies: Robert Schambier
Carol Hagel
Phil Smolik
Jack Lesar
Nora Ishibashi
Helen T. Bryant
Jo Ann Kawell
Deborah Brewster
Mary E. Bromage
Sheldon B. Silver
Patricia Miripol

Science: Ronald LeMay
Cynthia Talbert
Jeffrey Miripol
John Gloor
William Collien
Charles Nissim-Sabat

Reading: Timothy A. Foote
Raymond Traynor
Pamela D. Drell (Editor)

Mathematics: Jerry Howett

Project Assistance
Sara Plath

Graphic Art: Louise Hodges
Cover Design: Jeff Barnes

CONTENTS

TO THE LEARNER

HOW TO USE THIS BOOK

Building Basic Skills in Writing, Books 1 and 2 have been planned to give you what you need to master the basics of writing well.

BUILDING BASIC SKILLS IN WRITING	
Book 1	**Book 2**
Sentences	More About Sentences
Nouns	Punctuation
Verbs	Style
More About Verbs	Practical Writing
Pronouns	Spelling
Adjectives and Adverbs	

Together, the books give a complete program that is easy to use on your own or with a teacher in class.

Both books start with a short **Pre-Test.** The questions on the Pre-Test give you an idea of what you'll study in the book. They will also show you the writing skills you already have and those you need to build.

Both books end with a **Post-Test.** By taking the Post-Test after you have worked through the whole book, you will see how much your work has strengthened your skills. Use the **Test-Score Record** on page 14 to keep track of how you do on both Pre-Test and Post-Test.

You will find that *Building Basic Skills in Writing* is an easy, enjoyable way to study. All answers for the Pre-Test and Post-Test are given and explained. Answers to all of the exercises in the book start at the end of each unit. When you finish *Book 1,* you will have no problem moving right on to *Book 2.* Both books will give you all you need to strengthen your basic skills in writing.

WHAT ARE WRITING SKILLS?

Most writing skills are nothing more than common sense. This may surprise you if you have seen English grammar books with hundreds of rules for writing. But all these rules have one simple purpose: They help everyone write English in the same way. Then, what one person writes can be understood by everyone else.

There are differences between speaking and writing. When someone hears you speak, there are many ways to make what you say clear: the look on your face; the way you move your hands; the different ways you say things. From your voice alone, a person can tell if you are serious or if you are joking.

When other people read what you have written, there are none of these clues. The words themselves are all they see. For this reason, written words must be used more carefully than spoken words. Their meanings must be very clear so the reader can understand them. If you keep this idea in mind, many things in this book will be easier to learn.

A good way to learn writing skills is to read a lot. Read everything: school books, comic strips, newspapers, magazines, cereal boxes, advertisements. When you see a new word, write it down in a notebook and find it later in your dictionary. (It is a good idea to buy a dictionary if you don't have one.) Reread your notebook from time to time so you don't forget the new words.

Practice writing whenever you can. Write letters. Start a diary. The more you write, the better.

Writing skills are not hard to master. This book can teach you some of those skills. Your own ideas on writing can be just as important as the ones you will find in this book. Don't be afraid to ask why the rules are as they are. Make writing a part of your life.

The Editors at Contemporary Books

PRE-TEST

1 SENTENCES

Four groups of words tell a short story in each of the following questions. Read each group of words and look at the punctuation mark at the end of each group. One of these marks may be wrong. If so, put a check mark (✔) next to the number of the group of words whose punctuation is wrong. Check number 5 if there is no error.

1.   _____(1)   She asked him to dance?
     _____(2)   He said he'd love to.
     _____(3)   She was sorry.
     _____(4)   He kept stepping on her feet.
     _____(5)   no error

10. Ten <u>dollar's</u> worth of <u>gas</u> <u>can't</u> get us to <u>Ted's</u> house.

_____(1) dollar's

_____(2) gas

_____(3) can't

_____(4) Ted's

_____(5) no error

3 VERBS

Four words are underlined in each of the following sentences. If an error is underlined, put a check mark (✔) next to its number. If there is no error, check number 5.

11. He <u>ride</u> <u>to</u> work on the <u>same</u> bus <u>every</u> day.

_____(1) ride

_____(2) to

_____(3) same

_____(4) every

_____(5) no error

12. <u>Do</u> <u>oranges</u> and grapefruits <u>contain</u> <u>vitamin</u> C?

_____(1) Do

_____(2) oranges

_____(3) contain

_____(4) vitamin

_____(5) no error

13. <u>Was</u> <u>your</u> <u>parents</u> <u>born</u> in Puerto Rico?

_____(1) Was

_____(2) your

_____(3) parents

_____(4) born

_____(5) no error

14.   Bob <u>is</u> one <u>of</u> the people <u>who</u> <u>works</u> with me.

_____(1)   is
_____(2)   of
_____(3)   who
_____(4)   works
_____(5)   no error

15.   There <u>is</u> several <u>other</u> problems we <u>should</u> <u>talk</u> about.

_____(1)   is
_____(2)   other
_____(3)   should
_____(4)   talk
_____(5)   no error

4 MORE ABOUT VERBS

Four words are underlined in each sentence. If an error is underlined, put a check mark (✔) next to its number. If there is no error, check number 5.

16.   She <u>don't</u> <u>like</u> that <u>kind</u> of <u>talk</u>.

_____(1)   don't
_____(2)   like
_____(3)   kind
_____(4)   talk
_____(5)   no error

17.   We <u>come</u> yesterday <u>but</u> no one <u>was</u> home.

_____(1)   We
_____(2)   come
_____(3)   but
_____(4)   was
_____(5)   no error

___(4) them

___(5) no error

27. I don't know <u>hardly</u> <u>anything</u> about <u>it</u>.

___(1) don't

___(2) hardly

___(3) anything

___(4) it

___(5) no error

28. I like <u>this</u> pen, <u>because</u> it <u>writes</u> so <u>smooth</u>.

___(1) this

___(2) because

___(3) writes

___(4) smooth

___(5) no error

29. The dogs <u>are</u> <u>always</u> chasing <u>them</u> <u>pigeons</u>.

___(1) are

___(2) always

___(3) them

___(4) pigeons

___(5) no error

30. I think <u>this</u> <u>is</u> the <u>most</u> happiest day of <u>my</u> life.

___(1) this

___(2) is

___(3) most

___(4) my

___(5) no error

ANSWERS AND EXPLANATIONS—PRE-TEST

1 *Sentences*

1. (1) The sentence should end with a period.
2. (3) There should be no period. This is not the end of the sentence.
3. (5) no error
4. (3) Only an exclamation mark can make a sentence here.
5. (5) no error

2 *Nouns*

6. (3) Planets should not start with a capital letter.
7. (4) river should start with a capital letter.
8. (5) no error
9. (2) wive's should be wives.
10. (1) dollar's should be dollars'.

3 *Verbs*

11. (1) ride should be rides.
12. (5) no error
13. (1) was should be were.
14. (4) works should be work.
15. (1) is should be are.

4 *More About Verbs*

16. (1) don't should be doesn't.
17. (2) come should be came.
18. (2) done should be did.
19. (5) no error
20. (1) ain't should be haven't.

5 *Pronouns*

21. (4) your's should be yours.
22. (4) she should be her.
23. (2) me should be I.
24. (4) Theirselves should be themselves.
25. (5) no error

6 *Adjectives and Adverbs*

26. (1) This should be These or Those.
27. (2) hardly should not be used at all here.
28. (4) smooth should be smoothly.
29. (3) them should be the, these or those.
30. (3) most is not needed when happiest is used.

TEST SCORE RECORD

Fill in part of the chart after you take the Pre-Test. Write in the date of your Pre-Test at the bottom of the chart. Then work through the book before taking the Post-Test. After taking the Post-Test fill in the rest of the chart.

	SKILL UNITS	STUDY PAGES	TOTAL	PRE-TEST NUMBER RIGHT	POST-TEST NUMBER RIGHT
1	Sentences 1-5	15-47	5		
2	Nouns 6-10	48-74	5		
3	Verbs 11-15	75-100	5		
4	More About Verbs 16-20	101-136	5		
5	Pronouns 21-25	137-162	5		
6	Adjectives and Adverbs 26-30	163-179	5		
	TOTAL		30		
				(Date)	(Date)

1 SENTENCES

We have all met people who talk on and on. They never stop for an instant. Their words run together. You wonder when they find time to breathe. These people are hard to understand.

When most of us talk, we stop after a group of words before going on. This makes what we say easier to understand. Each group of words is called a **sentence.** In writing, we use certain marks to show where to stop if someone said the words out loud. These marks are called **punctuation marks.**

One of the most common punctuation marks is the period. The **period** is the dot that shows the end of a sentence. It is used in writing to mark places where we would stop for a moment.

Read the following story out loud. See how you stop at every period.

Mary was going home from work on the bus. It was very crowded and everyone was pressed tightly together. She felt something touching her hip. It felt like a man's hand. She wasn't sure. There was a man standing next to her. He was looking the other way. They were so close together that she couldn't see his hand. She wanted to move away but there was no room. When they reached the bus stop the man got off and she looked down. She laughed. She was holding her umbrella so the handle pressed against her hip.

Unless you read this story in a strange way, you had to stop at the periods. If you didn't, all the sentences would run into each other. The same thing is true of writing. If you leave the periods out of something you write, your work will be hard to read.

Here's another story. This time the periods have been left out. Read the story out loud.

> Karen's sister gave her an ugly sweater for her birthday Karen wanted to exchange it for something else at the store She called her sister and asked her where she bought it Her sister said she didn't buy it She had gotten it as a gift herself from their cousin Liz Karen called Liz and asked where she had bought it Liz said she hadn't bought it Someone gave it to her for her birthday Karen gave up on returning the sweater It was her friend Jane's anniversary next week She would give it to her

Now go back with a pen or pencil and put the periods in yourself. Can you tell where they should go? There should be 11 of them. Now read the story again below.

> Karen's sister gave her an ugly sweater for her birthday. Karen wanted to exchange it for something else at the store. She called her sister and asked her where she bought it. Her sister said she didn't buy it. She had gotten it as a gift herself from their cousin Liz. Karen called Liz and asked where she had bought it. Liz said she hadn't bought it either. Someone gave it to her for her birthday. Karen gave up on returning the sweater. It was her friend Jane's anniversary next week. She would give it to her.

THREE KINDS OF SENTENCES

The period is not the only punctuation mark that can end a sentence. There are two others. The question mark is one of them. It looks like this:

?

The third punctuation mark that can end a sentence is the exclamation mark. It looks like this:

!

Question marks are used after questions. Questions <u>ask</u> something.

> Excuse me. Do you have the time?
> Do I have what?
> The time.
> Do I look like a clock?

These six words will often start a sentence that is going to be a question: <u>WHO</u> <u>WHEN</u> <u>WHERE</u> <u>HOW</u> <u>WHAT</u> <u>WHY</u>

Add question marks at the end of each of these:

> Who is going to do this work __
> When will I ever find the time __
> Where do you want to start __
> How are you __
> What did he say __
> Why does love have to be so strange __

Exclamation marks are used after exclamations. An exclamation is something that when said out loud would be shouted. In newspaper offices, exclamation marks are called <u>screamers</u>.

> Shut up!
> Don't pull the trigger!

The bomb went: Tick. Tick. Tick. Tick. BOOM!

People who write advertisements often use exclamation marks so their ads will "shout" at the reader.

New! Improved! Best Ever!

Try not to use too many exclamation marks. They lose their punch. If you use only a few, they seem more powerful.

Exercise 1

Put a period, question mark, or exclamation mark after each sentence.

1. What time is it__
2. Help__
3. Are you asleep__
4. I'd like another cup, please__
5. Who does she think she is__
6. Stop or I'll shoot__

Check your answers before going on.

7. Fire__
8. How much does he weigh__
9. I think I'm falling asleep__
10. Will you marry me__
11. Can you hear me__
12. I'm screaming as loud as I can__

Answers start on page 40.

Exercise 2

The words that follow can be used to start questions. Read each beginning and add words to finish the sentences as questions. Be sure to end each with a question mark. On the line below your question, write another sentence that gives the answer. Be sure to end your second sentence with the right punctuation mark. The first is done as an example.

1. How much weight *do you want to lose?*
   I'd like to lose about 15 pounds.

2. Why do people _____
   _____

3. Who do the children _____
   _____

4. Where are _____
   _____

5. When do _____
   _____

6. How long will Al _____
   _____

7. Why did the _____
   _____

8. How much money _____
   _____

9. What time does _____
   _____

10. Which color _____
   _____

Answers start on page 40.

The end of a sentence is always shown by a period, question mark, or exclamation mark. The beginning of a sentence always has a capital letter.

She gave him a snapshot of herself.
Music makes the work go faster.

Exercise 3

The periods, question marks and one exclamation mark have been left out of this story. The capital letters at the beginning of each sentence have also been left out. Copy the story on the lines. Put in the punctuation marks and capital letters. Use only one exclamation mark in the whole story so that it has a powerful effect.

Nancy always visited her mother on Thursdays today was Thursday she didn't want to go Nancy's husband Tom had just lost his job again it was the second time in two months would her mother feel sorry for them no, her mother would spend the whole afternoon complaining about Tom why couldn't her mother mind her own business what a nasty old woman sometimes Nancy hated her mother maybe she should call and say she couldn't come

_____

_____

_____

_____

_____

_____

_____

_____

_____

_____

_____

_____

_____

_____

_____

_____

_____

_____

_____

_____

_____

_____

_____

Answers start on page 41.

COMPLETE SENTENCES

What do these groups of words mean?

Yellow.
Both of them.
Eight o'clock.

Maybe they are answers to questions.

What color is a ripe banana? Yellow.
Who ate with you? Both of them.
What time does it start? Eight o'clock.

People talk this way all the time. In writing, however, things must be clearer and easier to understand. The writer is not there to answer the reader's questions. To make writing as clear as possible, writers usually use <u>complete</u> sentences. Here are some complete sentences. Can you figure out what makes them complete?

> Ripe bananas are yellow.
> Both of them ate with us.
> It starts at eight o'clock.

Complete sentences must have two parts. One part is someone or something. The other part says what that someone or something <u>does</u>, or what that someone or something <u>is</u>. The first part is called the **subject.** The other part is called the **predicate.** Together these two parts make a complete sentence.

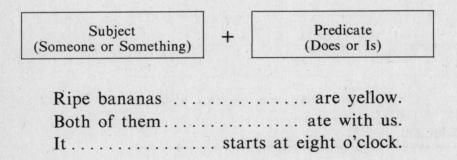

> Ripe bananas . . . . are yellow.
> Both of them . . . . ate with us.
> It . . . . starts at eight o'clock.

These would still be complete sentences with subjects and predicates if we add <u>not</u> to each predicate:

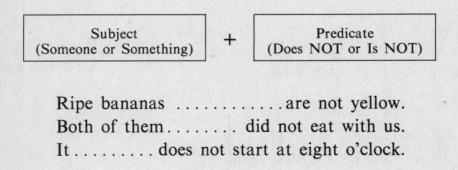

> Ripe bananas . . . . are not yellow.
> Both of them . . . . did not eat with us.
> It . . . . does not start at eight o'clock.

A **complete sentence** is a group of words with a subject and a predicate.

Exercise 4

Read this list of predicates. Then use them below to make five complete sentences. Don't forget to put punctuation marks at the end of each sentence. The first is done.

> . . .don't mix
> . . .equals four
> . . .will get you nowhere
> . . .is making everything cost more
> . . .weighed six pounds, ten ounces

1. Flattery *will get you nowhere*.

2. Inflation _____

3. Two plus two _____

4. Mrs. Rodriguez's baby _____

5. Water and oil _____

Here are some more predicates. Read each one. Then use them to make complete sentences. If you prefer, make up your own.

. . .will be the death of me	. . .is too expensive
. . .should be no problem	. . .is badly rusted
. . .got sick last Tuesday	. . .looks terrible
. . .can't hold his liquor	. . .is purple and green
. . .is jealous of her cousin	. . .is on at six o'clock
. . .ought to know better	. . .must be sore

6.   Your Uncle Jose _____

   _____

7.   Gerry's Chevrolet _____

   _____

8.   The A&P store _____

   _____

9.   His muscles _____

   _____

10.   Mark's custom van _____

   _____

11.   Her favorite TV show _____

   _____

12.   Mrs. Kithcart _____

   _____

13.   My landlord _____

   _____

14.   Getting up for work _____

   _____

15.   The woman in the laundry _____

   _____

Make up your own predicates for these. Don't forget the punctuation mark at the end of each sentence.

16.   Food stamps _____

   _____

17.   The paint in the kitchen _____

   _____

18. Nadine's daughter _____

_____

19. The phone bill _____

_____

20. My new record _____

_____

21. The police _____

_____

22. My favorite holiday _____

_____

23. Ziggy _____

_____

24. Denise _____

_____

25. Mr. Rivera _____

_____

Answers start on page 41.

SUBJECTS

We said before that the subject is someone or <u>something</u> that does or is. This something can be an idea, a condition, an activity, or a feeling. You can find the subject in a sentence by asking yourself, <u>who</u> or <u>what</u> does or is?

Subject	+	Predicate

Love . . . . doesn't last.
Learning . . . . can be a lifetime job.
Being overweight . . is bad for your health.

You could find the subject in the first sentence by asking, what doesn't last? You could find the subject in the second sentence by asking, what can be a lifelong job? You could find the third subject by asking, what is bad for your health?

So far all the subjects have been the first word or words in the sentence. This is not always so. Find the subject in this sentence:

> On July 4, the Smith family went to New Orleans.

Ask yourself, who or what went to New Orleans? The Smith family went to New Orleans. The Smith family is the subject of the sentence.

Exercise 5

Find the subjects in these sentences by asking yourself, who or what does or is? Then draw a line under the subjects. The first two have been done as examples.

1. Charlie was my best friend in the army. (Ask yourself, who was my best friend in the army?)

2. Without any doubt, bringing up children is hard. (Ask yourself, what is hard?)

3. The elephant escaped from its cage.

4. Defective merchandise may be returned within seven days.

5. John's mother is eighty years old.

6. That sweater must be dry cleaned.

Check your answers before going on.

7. Frank's son was arrested last night.

8. Bowling is a good way to relax.

9. Poverty is a problem in America.

10. Monroe struck out with bases loaded.

11. The bottom of the cake stuck to the pan.

12. Last Saturday night I got married.

Check your answers before going on.

13. Medical insurance can be an important thing.

14. That would be my guess.

15. The last worker went on strike at three in the morning.

16. Nevertheless I still believe him.

17. According to doctors, jogging is good for your heart.

18. Mrs. Pearlstein has two sons and a daughter.

Answers start on page 42.

Exercise 6

Rewrite the sentences shown in the last exercise. Make up new subjects to replace the ones in the book. Do this on your own sheet of paper. Here are examples of how you might do the first two.

1. The book said: Charlie was my best friend in the army. You could write: *The sergeant was my best friend in the army.*

2. The book said: The elephant escaped from its cage.
   You could write: *The snake escaped from its cage.*

SUBJECTS IN QUESTIONS

So far we have looked only at subjects in statements. A **statement** is a sentence that ends with a period. It tells something or makes a point. Sentences that ask **questions** also have subjects. Can you pick out the subjects in these questions?

Where is New York?
How old is Malcolm?
Will you be here Monday?

In the first question, the subject is New York; in the second, Malcolm; in the third, you. The easiest way to find the subjects in questions is to move the words around.

Subject	+	Predicate

New York . . . . is where?
Malcolm. . . . . is how old?
You . . . . will be here Monday?

If we put the sentences back the first way and underline the subjects, they look like this:

Where is New York?
How old is Malcolm?
Will you be here Monday?

Exercise 7

Turn these sentences around so you can find the subjects. Write the new sentences on the lines. Then underline the subjects in the first sentences. The first two have been done.

1. Where were <u>you</u>?

    You were where?

2. How can <u>anyone</u> stay awake in an English class?

    Anyone can stay awake in an English class how?

3. What did they do?

    _____

4. What kind of watch did you buy?

    _____

5. How does he put up with her?

    _____

6. When did the lights go out?

    _____

Check your answers before going on.

7. How did the fire start?

    _____

8. Why did he sell the bicycle?

    _____

9. How did the plate break?

    _____

10. Why haven't you paid your electric bill?

    _____

11.   Did he tell his wife the whole story?

_____

12.   How soon can supper be ready?

_____

Answers start on page 43.

SUBJECTS IN COMMANDS AND EXCLAMATIONS

There is a special kind of sentence that does not need a subject. This kind of sentence is called a **command**. It is neither a statement nor a question. It uses either a period or an exclamation mark. For example:

Leave me alone!
Please pass the salt.
Do it again.

A command is just what it sounds like: an order or a request telling someone to do something. The subject of a command is <u>always</u> the person it is said to, so there is no need to name the person in the sentence. If you wrote the subjects in the commands shown above, they could look like this:

Hey, you, leave me alone!
Hey, you, please pass the salt.
Hey, you, do it again.

The <u>hey</u> <u>you</u> is not needed. It is understood that the subject of every command is <u>you</u>.

The **exclamation** is even more special than the command. It doesn't need a subject <u>or</u> a predicate. It can be just a single word, or even a noise:

What a pretty dog!
Horsefeathers!
Huh!

Make up ten commands and write them on a separate sheet of paper.

Make up ten exclamations and write them on a separate sheet of paper.

PREDICATES

We said before that the predicate tells or asks what the subject <u>is</u> or <u>does</u>. Just because a group of words <u>mentions</u> doing or being something, however, does not make it a predicate. For example:

running a four minute mile

This group of words is more likely to be a subject than a predicate.

Running a four minute mile is hard.

In the sentence above, <u>running a four minute mile</u> is the subject. It answers the question, "<u>what</u> is hard?" To make it into a predicate, it must either be changed or have words added to it:

Michael <u>runs</u> a four minute mile.
                or
Michael <u>has</u> <u>been</u> running a four minute mile.

A predicate must do more than merely <u>mention</u> doing or being something. A predicate must <u>declare</u> or <u>ask</u> whether the subject does or is something.

Exercise 8

Write complete sentences which include the following groups of words as <u>subjects</u>. Start each sentence with a capital letter. Don't forget to put the right punctuation mark at the end of each sentence. The first two have been done as examples.

1. swimming the English Channel
    Swimming the English Channel isn't worth the effort.

2. singing in the shower
    Singing in the shower can be fun.

3. cooking hamburgers
    _____

4. getting pregnant
    _____

5. finding a bargain
    _____

6. looking for trouble
    _____

7. talking to strangers
    _____

8. falling in love
    _____

9. taking chances
    _____

10. winning one million dollars
    _____

Answers start on page 44.

Exercise 9

Write complete sentences which include the following groups of words as <u>predicates</u>. Don't forget to put punctuation marks at the ends of the sentences. The first two have been done as examples.

1. ... telling everyone what to do
   You are always telling everyone what to do.

2. ... getting to work late
   The boss said to stop getting to work late.

3. ... giving him the cold shoulder

4. ... defrosting the freezer

5. ... looking good

6. ... seething with rage

7. ... doing one hundred pushups

8. ... bleeding like a pig

9. ... saying I'm sorry

10. ... closing the store

Answers start on page 44.

FRAGMENTS

Why have we talked so much about complete sentences, subjects, and predicates? People often forget to make their sentences complete. Instead of writing complete sentences, they write only parts of them. A part of a complete sentence is called a **fragment**. Here are three examples of fragments:

Because he was ninety years old.
While waiting for the bus.
Crossing the street.

None of these fragments is a complete sentence. Let's look at them one by one and see why.

1. <u>Because he was ninety years old.</u> Because he was ninety years old, <u>what</u>? What happened because he was ninety years old? Here is a complete sentence:

Because he was ninety years old, he could do only fifty pushups.

Another way to make this group of words into a complete sentence is to take away the word <u>because</u>:

He was ninety years old.

2. <u>While waiting for the bus.</u> <u>What</u> happened while <u>who</u> was waiting for the bus? Here is a way to make this a complete sentence:

While waiting for the bus, he met Linda.

3. <u>Crossing</u> the <u>street</u>. What about it? These would be complete sentences:

> Mitchell was crossing the street.
>
> or
>
> Crossing the street can be fatal.

Exercise 10

Each of the following groups of words is either a complete sentence or a fragment. If the group is a complete sentence, write "C" for <u>complete</u> in the space. If it is a fragment, write "F" for <u>fragment</u>. The first two have been done.

1. On Monday night at Sam's house.   *F*
2. Bill slept poorly.   *C*
3. Be patient.   _____
4. Since France is so far from England.   _____
5. Because so many people pay bills late.   _____
6. How fast can you go?   _____
7. Winning is not everything.   _____
8. Selma dropped a rubber band.   _____
9. We will be there tomorrow.   _____
10. Waiting on line at the unemployment office.   _____

Check your answers before going on.

11. Harold will change her diapers. _____

12. You're not listening to me. _____

13. Please try to stay awake. _____

14. Unless something happens. _____

15. Be there. _____

16. How much does it cost to replace the clutch? _____

17. Fixing the brakes. _____

18. Lilah always has fresh flowers in her kitchen. _____

19. Once in a lifetime. _____

20. Please give me a hand with this. _____

Check your answers before going on.

21. They've been dancing for five hours. _____

22. Just a few minutes more. _____

23. Circumstances like these. _____

24. I don't doubt it for an instant. _____

25. Applying for a loan from the bank. _____

26. Could you please repeat that? _____

27. What? _____

28. Stop! _____

29. Nothing you'd be interested in. _____

30. Shopping on Saturday afternoons. _____

Answers start on page 45.

Exercise 11

Add words to these sentence fragments to make them complete sentences. Don't forget to use punctuation marks at the end of each sentence. Start each sentence with a capital letter.

1. lying in court
    Lying in court is a crime.

2. life in prison
    If you haven't been there, you know nothing about life in prison.

3. because he was too young

4. although she came from Kansas

5. after covering his face with kisses

6. nothing but bills

7. only on Sundays

8. how fast you can go

9. scratching a mosquito bite

10. shaving with a rusty blade

11. trying over and over again

12. in order to remove the stain

_____

13. the only friend she has

_____

14. straightening his tie

_____

15. the lion on the left

_____

16. trying to take him seriously

_____

17. waking up from a nightmare

_____

18. if you freeze leftovers

_____

19. even if you apologize

_____

20. taking aspirin

_____

Answers start on page 45.

REVIEW EXERCISE—SENTENCES

Add the correct punctuation mark after each group of words. If the group of words is a statement, add a period. If it is a question, add a question mark. If it is an exclamation, add an exclamation mark. If the group of words is a fragment, don't add any punctuation mark. Write **statement, question, exclamation,** or **fragment** in the blanks to name each group of words.

1. How strange _____

2. Do you have the time _____

3. After due consideration _____

4. You must be joking _____

5. Is Sidney taking dance lessons _____

6. The weather will be warmer
   tomorrow _____

7. Martha left _____

8. Can you reach the switch from
   there _____

9. Speaking as frankly as possible _____

10. If you haven't heard _____

11. How can they manage on so
    little money _____

12. Unless you have a better idea _____

13. What nerve _____

14. Will that be cash or charge _____

15. It will be her third marriage _____

16. Without the slightest doubt _____

17. Last Thursday at six o'clock _____

18. Ouch _____

19. Could you give me a hand _____

20. I'm sorry _____

21. The paint is still wet _____

22. While washing the dishes _____

23. They agreed to invite the whole
    family _____

24. Where does the bus leave from _____

25. Are you Mrs. Mendez _____

ANSWERS AND EXPLANATIONS—SENTENCES

Exercise 1

1. What time is it?
2. Help!
3. Are you asleep?
4. I'd like another cup, please.
5. Who does she think she is?
6. Stop or I'll shoot. or !

7. Fire!
8. How much does he weigh?
9. I think I'm falling asleep.
10. Will you marry me?
11. Can you hear me?
12. I'm screaming as loud as I can!

Exercise 2

You could have finished the questions and written your answers in many different ways. Here are some examples. Make sure you ended the questions with question marks. Did you end answers with periods?

1. How much weight do you want to lose?
   I'd like to lose about 15 pounds.
2. Why do people sleep in church?
   They probably fell asleep because it was hot inside.
3. Who do the children need to be with?
   A child needs his whole family.
4. Where are my black socks?
   I really don't know, dear.

5. When do we eat?
   We can sit down as soon as you make the salad.
6. How long will Al wait for his girl?
   He says he'll wait forever.
7. Why did the club break up?
   They decided to give up the idea.
8. How much money will you get from your Christmas club next year?
   If I pay $10 every two weeks, I'll get back $260.
9. What time does your favorite show come on?
   It starts at 8:00.
10. Which color looks best with this shirt?
   I like blue.

Exercise 3

Nancy always visited her mother on Thursdays. Today was Thursday. She didn't want to go. Nancy's husband Tom had just lost his job again. It was the second time in two months. Would her mother feel sorry for them? No, her mother would spend the whole afternoon complaining about Tom. Why couldn't her mother mind her own business? What a nasty old woman! Sometimes Nancy hated her mother. Maybe she should call and say she couldn't come.

Exercise 4

1. Flattery will get you nowhere.
2. Inflation is making everything cost more.
3. Two plus two equals four.
4. Mrs. Rodriguez's baby weighed six pounds, ten ounces.
5. Water and oil don't mix.

There are many ways to make complete sentences. You

could have used the list or made up your own. Here are some samples.

6. Your Uncle Jose is jealous of her cousin.
7. Gerry's Chevrolet is badly rusted.
8. The A&P store sells meat, milk, vegetables, and candy.
9. His muscles must be sore.
10. Mark's custom van is purple and green.
11. Her favorite TV show is on at six o'clock.
12. Mrs. Kithcart got sick last Tuesday.
13. My landlord ought to know better.
14. Getting up for work will be the death of me.
15. The woman in the laundry looks terrible.

Here are examples of one way predicates could have been added to make complete sentences.

16. Food stamps are taken at the store.
17. The paint in the kitchen is dry.
18. Nadine's daughter had a baby last week.
19. The phone bill still has to be paid.
20. My new record is great.
21. The police are on strike.
22. My favorite holiday is Christmas.
23. Ziggy is taking judo lessons.
24. Denise went to Des Moines last week.
25. Mr. Rivera is cheerful this morning.

Exercise 5

1. Charlie was my best friend in the army.
2. Without any doubt, bringing up children is hard.
3. The elephant escaped from its cage.
4. Defective merchandise may be returned within seven days.
5. John's mother is eighty years old.
6. That sweater must be dry cleaned.

7. Frank's son was arrested last night.
8. Bowling is a good way to relax.
9. Poverty is a problem in America.
10. Monroe struck out with bases loaded.
11. The bottom of the cake stuck to the pan.
12. Last Saturday night I got married.

13. Medical insurance can be an important thing.
14. That would be my guess.
15. The last worker went on strike at three in the morning.
16. Nevertheless I still believe him.
17. According to doctors, jogging is good for your heart.
18. Mrs. Pearlstein has two sons and a daughter.

Exercise 6

There are many ways you could have rewritten this exercise.
Check yours with a friend.

Exercise 7

1. Where were you?
    You were where?
2. How can anyone stay awake in an English class?
    Anyone can stay awake in an English class how?
3. What did they do?
    They did do what?
4. What kind of watch did you buy?
    You did buy what kind of watch?
5. How does he put up with her?
    He does put up with her how?
6. When did the lights go out?
    The lights did go out when?

7.   How did the fire start?
     The fire did start how?

8.   Why did he sell the bicycle?
     He did sell the bicycle why?

9.   How did the plate break?
     The plate did break how?

10.   Why haven't you paid your electric bill?
      You haven't paid your electric bill why?

11.   Did he tell his wife the whole story?
      He did tell his wife the whole story?

12.   How soon can supper be ready?
      Supper can be ready how soon?

Exercise 8

There are many ways to use the groups of words as subjects of sentences. Here are some samples. Your sentences can be different, but you must use the group of words as a subject.

1.   Swimming the English Channel isn't worth the effort.
2.   Singing in the shower can be fun.
3.   Cooking hamburgers does not pay well.
4.   Getting pregnant may come as a surprise.
5.   Finding a bargain is always fun.
6.   Looking for trouble leads to bad luck.
7.   Talking to strangers can be dangerous.
8.   Falling in love is better the second time around.
9.   Taking chances sometimes pays off.
10.   Winning one million dollars doesn't happen every day.

Exercise 9

Again, there are many ways to use each group of words.
Here are some samples. Your sentences can be different, but

you must have used each group of words as part of the predicate of a sentence.

1. You are always telling everyone what to do.
2. The boss said to stop getting to work late.
3. All his friends started giving him the cold shoulder.
4. My sister hates defrosting the freezer.
5. Pam was really looking good in her bathing suit.
6. Rudolph was seething with rage.
7. He must still be doing one hundred pushups every morning.
8. The knife slipped and Sam started bleeding like a pig.
9. I hate saying I'm sorry.
10. He will be closing the store late tonight.

Exercise 10

1. F	11. C	21. C
2. C	12. C	22. F
3. C	13. C	23. F
4. F	14. F	24. C
5. F	15. C	25. F
6. C	16. C	26. C
7. C	17. F	27. C
8. C	18. C	28. C
9. C	19. F	29. F
10. F	20. C	30. F

Exercise 11

Your sentences will probably be different from these. Make sure they are complete.

1. Lying in court is a crime.

2. If you haven't been there, you know nothing about life in prison.
3. They stopped him at the door because he was too young.
4. Although she came from Kansas, she loved living in Mexico.
5. After covering his face with kisses, she fainted.
6. My mail is nothing but bills.
7. They go out running only on Sundays.
8. Do they know how fast you can go?
9. Scratching a mosquito bite will leave a scar.
10. Why don't you stop shaving with a rusty blade?
11. I'm sick of trying over and over again.
12. In order to remove the stain use a little fresh lemon juice.
13. Marva is the only friend she has.
14. While straightening his tie, she gave him a wink.
15. The lion on the left is bigger than that leopard.
16. I'm forever trying to take him seriously.
17. Waking up from a nightmare is like being saved just in time.
18. If you freeze leftovers, you can eat them for lunch.
19. I'll never forgive you even if you apologize.
20. Try taking aspirin and going to bed.

ANSWERS AND EXPLANATIONS—REVIEW EXERCISE

1. How strange!   exclamation
2. Do you have the time?   question
3. After due consideration   fragment
4. You must be joking.   statement
            or   or
    You must be joking!   exclamation

5.	Is Sidney taking dance lessons?	question
6.	The weather will be warmer tomorrow.	statement
7.	Martha left.	statement
8.	Can you reach the switch from there?	question
9.	Speaking as frankly as possible	fragment
10.	If you haven't heard	fragment
11.	How can they manage on so little money?	question
12.	Unless you have a better idea	fragment
13.	What nerve!	exclamation
14.	Will that be cash or charge?	question
15.	It will be her third marriage.	statement
16.	Without the slightest doubt	fragment
17.	Last Thursday at six o'clock	fragment
18.	Ouch!	exclamation
19.	Could you give me a hand?	question
20.	I'm sorry.	statement
21.	The paint is still wet.	statement
22.	While washing the dishes	fragment
23.	They agreed to invite the whole family.	statement
24.	Where does the bus leave from?	question
25.	Are you Mrs. Mendez?	question

2 NOUNS

WHAT IS A NOUN?

A **noun** is a word which names a person, animal, place or thing.

Why should anyone care whether or not a word is a noun?

The reason is that only nouns can do certain jobs in sentences. For example, only a noun will fill the blank in the following sentence:

I don't want your _____.

If you can find a word which completes the sentence, but is not a noun, the publisher of this book will send you an unabridged dictionary free.

Exercise 1

Find 15 different nouns which complete the above sentence. The first three have been done as examples.

I don't want your _____.

1. *sweater*   6. _____   11. _____

2. *sister*   7. _____   12. _____

3. *advice*   8. _____   13. _____

4. _____   9. _____   14. _____

5. _____   10. _____   15. _____

Answers start on page 69.

Exercise 2

Fill the blanks in the following story with nouns. Remember that a noun is a word that names a person, animal, place, or thing.

> Jane had the biggest _____ of any-
> one who lived in our town. It was so big that
> she had to carry it in a _____. It would
> not fit in a _____. Tom Crowley, the
> town barber, liked it so much that he offered
> to give Jane two _____ for it. Jane
> turned him down. Charlie Poole, the town
> _____, offered Jane half a dozen
> _____. She refused that offer, too. One
> day a man came to town from _____
> and stole Jane's _____. The man's name
> was _____. He was a real _____.

Answers start on page 69.

WHAT NOUNS DO

If someone asked you what a shovel is, you could answer in several ways. The obvious way would be to describe one. This would not be as easy as you might think. Shovels come in all shapes and sizes. They are made from metal, plastic, fiberglass, and wood. They can be of every color.

Instead of trying to describe shovels we could simply say what they are used for: shovels are tools used to dig or scoop up soil, coal, and similar substances. And in fact, most dictionaries define shovel in just this way.

When we try to describe nouns as words that name persons, animals, places, or things, we run into the same problem. Advice is a noun, but is advice really a thing? God is a noun, but is God really a person?

Instead of trying to describe all nouns, we can simply say what they are used for, just as we did with shovels.

Nouns are used as the subjects of sentences.

Examples: <u>English</u> is understood throughout the world.
<u>God</u> saw that it was good.

The subject has been left out of the following sentence, so a noun is required to complete it:

_____ is a pain in the neck.

<u>Terry</u> is a pain in the neck.

<u>Studying</u> is a pain in the neck.

Since they are subjects, <u>Terry</u> and <u>studying</u> are nouns.

We can also fill in the blank with groups of words. Groups of words are called **phrases.**

<u>The girl</u> is a pain in the neck.

<u>The other girl</u> is a pain in the neck.

<u>The loud, talkative girl</u> is a pain in the neck.

<u>The girl who hit me</u> is a pain in the neck.

<u>The girl who is sitting down</u> is a pain in the neck.

These phrases are doing a noun's job, so they are called **noun phrases.**

Exercise 3

Make up subjects using noun phrases with two words, three words, four words, five words, and six words to complete this sentence:

_____ is my favorite.

1. _____ _____ is my favorite.

2. _____ _____ _____ is my favorite.

3. _____ _____ _____ _____ is my favorite.

4. _____ _____ _____ _____ _____ is my favorite.

5. _____ _____ _____ _____ _____ _____ is my favorite.

Answers start on page 69.

THE ARTICLE TEST

There is another way to tell if a word is a noun. You can put an **article** before it as a test.

Articles are the words <u>a</u>, <u>an</u>, <u>some</u>, and <u>the</u>. You can put an article before most nouns.

Examples: <u>an</u> egg

<u>the</u> doctor

<u>some</u> happiness

You have to be careful with the article test because there are often words between the article and noun which are not nouns. In the following examples, only the last word in each phrase is a noun.

Examples: <u>the</u> most important <u>ideas</u>

<u>a</u> fat old <u>pig</u>

<u>some</u> happier and richer <u>men</u>

Exercise 4

Underline the nouns in the following passage. Remember that a noun usually names a person, animal, place, or thing.

When in doubt, try putting an article before the word. The first three have been done as examples.

A <u>feedlot</u> is a <u>farm</u> where young <u>cattle</u> are fattened for slaughter. To make the most money, farmers want the animals to grow as quickly as possible on the least amount of food. The young cattle are penned in a small place so they won't lose weight by running around. Hundreds or even thousands of animals stand up to their ankles in dung. You can smell a feedlot from miles away.

Answers start on page 70.

OBJECTS

You already know that nouns can be used as the subjects of sentences, but they can do more than that. Let's look again at the sentence we used in the first exercise in this chapter:

I don't want your _____.

A noun is missing from this sentence, but it is not the subject. The subject of the sentence is <u>I</u>. The missing word here is part of the predicate. The missing part is called the <u>object</u>.

Here are other examples of objects:

Examples: He kicked <u>the bottle</u> into the street.

I like <u>wine</u>, but I love <u>beer</u>.

Did Sheri tell you <u>the story</u>?

Can you make up a definition of an object based on these examples?

According to grammar books, objects are the word or words that <u>receive</u> the action of a verb. **Objects** are nouns or noun phrases.

Another way to think of objects is this: The subject <u>does</u>, and the object is <u>done to</u>.

Michelle gave a boring speech.

Michelle is the subject here. She is the one who gave the boring speech (the object).

Exercise 5

Underline the objects in these sentences. The first two have been done for you.

1. Claude threw <u>the newspaper</u> away.

2. The president signed <u>the bill</u>.

3. She finished her work very quickly.

4. The union won the strike.

5. Do you really believe commercials?

6. Inflation hurts workers most.

7. Who left the radio on?

8. She bought too much meat.

Check your answers before going on.

9. The dog hurt its foot.

10. The store is having a sale.

11. Uncle Gerry filled his cup.

12.   When does the postman bring the mail?

13.   Lightning struck the steeple again and again.

14.   The box scratched the table.

15.   Annette signed her name carefully.

Answers start on page 70.

There are different kinds of objects, and a sentence can have more than one.

Examples: They told my aunt the whole story.
We sold the car to our cousin.
They gave Sheila her present at her house.

Exercise 6

Underline the objects in these sentences. The first two have been done for you.

1.   He always brings his mother a gift.

2.   That teacher never taught his students a single thing.

3.   Has he shown the pictures to his children yet?

4.   Give your husband a big kiss.

5.   Stay away from my husband.

6.   He packed his socks, suits, toothbrush, and shirts, but forgot his ticket.

7.   Ernesto gave his brother the keys.

8.   She's afraid to ask her mother for help.

Check your answers before going on.

9. Charlie wrote me a letter.

10. Alvin has stayed away from liquor.

11. Did Patricia warn Jack about the noise?

12. You should ask your boss for a raise.

13. Marti gave her old baby clothes to her sister.

14. Mail your check or money order to the following address.

15. Did Carmen offer Maria some free advice?

Answers start on page 71.

COMMON AND PROPER NOUNS

You've probably noticed that some nouns are always capitalized, but others are not. Nouns which always start with a capital letter are called proper nouns; others are called common nouns. Of course, any noun that starts a sentence will be capitalized.

proper nouns	common nouns

Pete Steele	person
French	language
France	country
Mount Everest	mountain
Marlboros	cigarettes
January	month

proper nouns	common nouns

Monday   day
The Revolutionary War   war

Common nouns can refer to many things; proper nouns are meant to refer to only one. There are four billion persons on our planet, but when you say Pete Steele you mean only one of them. There are hundreds of languages, but only one of them is French. There are many brands of cigarettes, but only one is called Marlboro. The names of specific days, months, and historical events always start with capital letters.

The same noun can be common and proper, depending on how it is used.

Examples: Richard Nixon was president in 1971.

The saddest of all was President Richard Nixon.

In the first sentence, president is a common noun. There have been many presidents. In the second sentence, however, President is a title, part of Nixon's name. Words like president are capitalized only when they are part of someone's name.

Examples: mayor   Mayor Gibbs
lady   Lady Wellington
doctor   Dr. Greene
king   King George

Exercise 7

If the underlined word is correct, write "correct" on the line. If the word is wrong, write it correctly. The first three have been done for you.

1. The best <u>Doctor</u> in town is Dr. Greene.   *doctor*

2. Dr. Greene drives a big red <u>cadillac</u>.   *Cadillac*

3. He speaks <u>English</u> with an accent.   *correct*

4. It took sixteen days to climb the <u>Mountain</u>.   _____

5. Jupiter and <u>Saturn</u> are the largest planets.   _____

6. The president met with <u>mayor</u> Stevenson today.   _____

7. The Hudson River, like the <u>Mississippi</u>, empties into the Atlantic Ocean.   _____

8. Dr. Oliver's <u>Nurse</u> is middle-aged.   _____

Check your answers before going on.

9. The <u>Japanese</u> make some excellent cameras.   _____

10. The lieutenant gave <u>private</u> Johnston his orders.   _____

11. They were married in a civil ceremony by a <u>Judge</u>.   _____

12. If I had the money, I'd buy a <u>porsche</u>.   _____

13. The <u>Coast</u> of New Jersey runs south-
     west.   _____

14. He is originally from <u>north</u> Dakota.   _____

15. I thought we agreed on <u>Wednesday</u>.   _____

Answers start on page 71.

PLURALS

Most nouns have two forms. The first form refers to one person or thing; the second form refers to two or more. These forms are called <u>singular</u> and <u>plural</u>.

singular	plural
one picture	two picture<u>s</u>
a dog	some dog<u>s</u>
an egg	some egg<u>s</u>

We write one <u>picture</u>, but two <u>pictures</u>. <u>Pictures</u> is the plural form of <u>picture</u>.

Most nouns form their plurals by adding s, but there are exceptions. Here are the most common exceptions:

1. **Nouns which end in <u>s</u>, <u>sh</u>, <u>ch</u>, <u>x</u>, or <u>z</u>, add -es to form their plurals.**

Use this rule to write plural forms of the following nouns.

a kiss   some   *kisses*   the bus   some   _____

one brush   five   _____   a crush   two   _____

a couch   two   _____   one pouch   six   _____

one box   some   _____   the fox   some   _____

Here's a little jingle to remind you of these letters:

Short **s**ick **z**ebras **X**-ray **ch**eaper.

The reason for this rule is that without the e̲, the plurals would sound the same as the singulars. How could you say kisss̲ so it sounded different from kiss̲? Adding -es makes the plural sound different.

2. Some nouns that end in y̲ form their plurals by adding s̲:

Use this rule to write plural forms of the following nouns.

a day	five	_days_
one key	some	_____
an alloy	some	_____

Most nouns which end in y̲, however, drop the y̲ and add ie̲s̲:

Use this rule to write plural forms, of the following nouns.

a story	some	_stories_
one try	two	_____
one baby	six	_____

How can you tell which plurals end with y̲s̲ and which end with ie̲s̲? The plural ends with y̲s̲ only when the y̲ follows a vowe̲l̲. Vowels are the letters a̲, e̲, i̲, o̲, u̲.

Here's a little jingle to remind you of the vowels:

Aunt **E**llen **i**s **o**ften **u**nwanted.

3. Some nouns that end with o form plurals by adding -es:

Use this rule to write plural forms of the following nouns.

a tomato	some	_tomatoes_
one potato	two	_____ ,
the hero	some	_____

4. Many nouns which end with f or fe form the plural with ves:

Use this rule to form plurals of the following nouns.

a knife	some	_knives_
the wife	six	_____
one life	nine	_____
a leaf	some	_____

Here are some exceptions. Add only an s.

a chief	some	_chiefs_
one puff	two	_____
the cliff	some	_____
the cuff	some	_____

If you are unsure about an f or fe word, check in the dictionary.

5. Some nouns change their vowels or add an irregular ending to form their plurals.

Match the following nouns by drawing a line from the singular to the plural forms. The first is done as an example.

man   women
child   teeth
mouse   feet
woman   children
foot   mice
tooth   men

6. Some nouns have the same form in both singular and plural.

Use this rule to write plural forms of the following nouns.

one deer   eight _____ *deer* _____

one sheep   six _____

a fish   some _____

Exercise 8

Write the plurals of the following singular nouns.

1. child ____ *children* ____
2. horse _____
3. day _____
4. city _____
5. sheep _____

6. potato _____
7. boss _____
8. march _____
9. mouse _____
10. policeman _____

Write the singulars of the following plural nouns.

1. skies _____   6. loaves _____

2. foxes _____   7. teeth _____

3. puppies _____   8. losses _____

4. feet _____   9. women _____

5. fish _____   10. wishes _____

Answers start on page 72.

COUNT NOUNS AND MASS NOUNS

Some nouns do not have plurals. As you can tell from the following conversation, Sam does not know this.

Sam: Did you have a good time?
George: We had fun.
Sam: How many funs did you have?
George: Funs? You don't know much English, do you Sam?
Sam: Sure I do. I know thousands of Englishes.

Sam is wrong, of course. He does not know much English. Funs and Englishes are not real words; fun and English have no plural forms.

Words like fun and English are called mass nouns. Mass nouns cannot be counted. You can speak little English or much English, but no one can speak ten English.

Other nouns, which can be counted, are called count nouns.

Examples:

mass nouns

count nouns

cash   dollar
furniture   chair
luck   accident
courage   lion

The reason you must know the difference between mass nouns and count nouns is that <u>much</u> and <u>little</u> go before mass nouns, but <u>many</u> and <u>few</u> go before count nouns. (<u>A lot of</u> goes before both kinds.)

Examples: Right: I don't have <u>much</u> cash.

Wrong: I don't have <u>many</u> cash.

Right: He has <u>little</u> courage.

Wrong: He has <u>few</u> courage.

Right: <u>Few</u> lions like asparagus.

Wrong: <u>Little</u> lions like asparagus.

Notice that in the last example, both sentences make sense, but the word <u>little</u> changes the meaning.

Exercise 9

Fill in the blanks with the correct word. Remember that <u>few</u> and <u>many</u> go with count nouns; <u>little</u> and <u>much</u> go with mass nouns. The first one has been done as an example.

1. <u>Few</u> people believe the politicians will do anything about unemployment. (Few/Little)

2. How _____ air is left in the tank? (many/much)

3. Their baby knows _____ words for its age. (many/much)

4. Taking an elephant on a trip is _____ trouble if you plan carefully. (few/little)

5. _____ dollars add up to a lot of cash. (Many/Much)

6. She had _____ little problems but _____ big ones. (many/much) (few/little)

7. _____ problems are so difficult to solve. (Few/Little)

8. There are too _____ cars on the road at rush hour. (many/much)

9. Dora has too _____ chairs and too _____ other furniture. (many/much) (few/little).

10. _____ people would say Ron has _____ courage. (Many/Much) (many/much)

Answers start on page 73.

POSSESSIVE NOUNS

If Cynthia has a coat, we call it: <u>Cynthia's</u> coat.

<u>Cynthia's</u> is the **possessive** form of the noun <u>Cynthia</u>.

Here are some other examples:

Examples: a month's pay
the woman's husband
my uncle's friend's sister's house

Not all nouns form the possessive by adding 's. Compare these two sentences:

1. The children slept in the girl's room.
2. The children slept in the girls' room.

The only difference between the two sentences is the words girl's and girls': the **apostrophes** are in slightly different places. But the sentences mean different things. The children in the first sentence may have slept in a bedroom; the children in the second sentence may have slept in a restroom. How can moving a punctuation mark make such a big difference?

Girl's is the possessive form of the singular noun girl. A girl's room means her bedroom or her classroom. Girls', however, is the possessive form of the plural noun girls. A girls' room means a restroom used by girls, as a men's room is used by men or a ladies' room by women.

As you can see, where you put the apostrophe can make a great deal of difference. By putting it in the right place, you give the reader much information; by putting it in the wrong place, you can mislead people. Here are the rules:

1. All singular nouns form their possessives by adding 's.

America's victory
a dog's life

Singular nouns add 's even when they already end with s.

the boss's desk
Mr. Jones's wife

(Some books and newspapers only add an apostrophe to singular nouns which already end with s, sh, ch, z, and x, but you will always be correct if you add 's to any singular noun.

2.   **Plural nouns which end with s just add an apostrophe.**

        many students' books
        two years' time
        the horses' heads

Plural nouns that do not end with s add 's, just like singular nouns.

        men's room
        children's clothes
        people's fears

Exercise 10

Write the correct possessive ending in the blank spaces after the nouns in the following sentences. The first one has been done as an example.

1. Many doctors' bills are too high.

2. The movie_____ ending was sad.

3. Try not to stare at Doris_____ scar.

4. Most boys_____ worries are the same.

5. Women_____ shoes are sold on the fourth floor.

6. It's colder than the hair on a polar bear_____ back.

7. We'll see you again after New Year_____ Eve.

8. This is only three week_____ worth of dirt.

Check your answers before going on.

9. Both of Lisa____ brother____ wives will be there.

10. Max____ mother lives in Joan____ building.

11. This house____ roof leaks.

12. This was my grandmother____ pin.

13. May I please have five dollar____ worth?

14. It's a dog____ life.

15. Elephant____ brains are larger than people____.

Answers start on page 73.

REVIEW EXERCISE—NOUNS

This exercise will show how much you learned about nouns. Something is wrong with each sentence. Rewrite each sentence on the line below it so that it is correct.

1. The mississippi river runs down to the sea.

   _____

2. Only sharp knifes cut tomatos easily.

   _____

3. Much accidents could be avoided.

   _____

4. Emily was tired of picking up her childrens' toys.

   _____

5. In 1974 Cockburn became Mayor of Pillburg.

   _____

6. The boys spent hours learning to catch flys with their hands.

   _____

7.   Much marriages end in divorce.

_____

8.   The federal governments's welfare programs are not adequate.

_____

_____

9.   Matchs must be kept away from small children.

_____

10.   What should you do when two week's pay goes in one?

_____

ANSWERS AND EXPLANATIONS—NOUNS

Exercise 1

Any words which you have found that finish the sentence are nouns. Here are some more examples of nouns:

1.	sweater	6.	money	11.	flowers
2.	sister	7.	freedom	12.	hillside
3.	advice	8.	apples	13.	city
4.	breakfast	9.	guitar	14.	letter
5.	respect	10.	turtle	15.	ability

Exercise 2

Any words which you have found that fit in the blanks are nouns. Here is one way the story could be completed:

> Jane had the biggest pigeon of anyone who lived in our town. It was so big that she had to carry it in a wheelbarrow. It would not fit in a birdcage. Tom Crowley, the town barber, liked it so much that he offered to give Jane two canaries for it. Jane turned him down. Charlie Poole, the town drunk, offered Jane half a dozen diamonds. She refused that offer, too. One day a man came to town from Nebraska and stole Jane's pigeon. The man's name was Quiggs. He was a real thief.

Exercise 3

Any phrases you made up that finish the sentences are

correct answers. Here are some possible right answers:

1. That <u>one</u> is my favorite.
2. The <u>orange one</u> is my favorite.
3. That <u>one over there</u> is my favorite.
4. The <u>one you don't like</u> is my favorite.
5. The <u>one that makes you sick</u> is my favorite.

Exercise 4

A <u>feedlot</u> is a <u>farm</u> where young <u>cattle</u> are fattened for <u>slaughter</u>. To make the most <u>money</u>, <u>farmers</u> want the <u>animals</u> to grow as quickly as possible on the least <u>amount</u> of <u>food</u>. The young <u>cattle</u> are penned in a small <u>place</u> so they won't lose <u>weight</u> by running around. <u>Hundreds</u> or even <u>thousands</u> of <u>animals</u> stand up to their <u>ankles</u> in <u>dung</u>. You can smell a <u>feedlot</u> from <u>miles</u> away.

Exercise 5

1. Claude threw <u>the newspaper</u> away.
2. The president signed <u>the bill</u>.
3. She finished <u>her work</u> very quickly.
4. The union won <u>the strike</u>.
5. Do you really believe <u>commercials</u>?
6. Inflation hurts <u>workers</u> most.
7. Who left <u>the radio</u> on?
8. She bought <u>too much meat</u>.

9. The dog hurt its foot.
10. The store is having a sale.
11. Uncle Gerry filled his cup.
12. When does the postman bring the mail?
13. Lightning struck the steeple again and again.
14. The box scratched the table.
15. Annette signed her name carefully.

Exercise 6

1. He always brings his mother a gift.
2. That teacher never taught his students a single thing.
3. Has he shown the pictures to his children yet?
4. Give your husband a big kiss.
5. Stay away from my husband.
6. He packed his socks, suits, toothbrush and shirts, but forgot his ticket.
7. Ernesto gave his brother the keys.
8. She's afraid to ask her mother for help.
9. Charlie wrote me a letter.
10. Alvin has stayed away from liquor.
11. Did Patricia warn Jack about the noise?
12. You should ask your boss for a raise.
13. Marti gave her old baby clothes to her sister.
14. Mail your check or money order to the following address.
15. Did Carmen offer Maria some free advice?

Exercise 7

1. doctor. Doctor is capitalized only at the beginning of a sentence, or when it is part of a person's name.

2. Cadillac. Only one make of car is called Cadillac. It is a proper noun.

3. Correct. Names of languages are always proper nouns.

4. mountain. Only names of specific mountains are proper nouns.

5. Correct. Only one planet is named Saturn. It is a proper noun.

6. Mayor. Mayor must begin with a capital letter here. It is used as a name. Mayor Stevenson is a proper noun.

7. Correct. The underlined word is a specific river. There is only one. It is a proper noun and must start with a capital letter.

8. nurse. The word is not used as part of a name. It is a common noun and does not need a capital letter.

9. Correct. Here we are speaking of a specific group of people whose nationality is Japanese. Words for a person's nationality must always begin with a capital letter.

10. Private. Private Johnston is used as a proper noun. It must start with a capital letter.

11. judge. The judge is not named. This is a common noun. It does not start with a capital letter.

12. Porsche. This is a proper noun. It must begin with a capital letter.

13. coast. This word is a common noun. It does not need to start with a capital letter.

14. North. North Dakota is a state of the U.S. All states begin with capital letters, even those with two words.

15. Correct. Days of the week, like months of the year, must start with capital letters.

Exercise 8: Plurals

1. children
2. horses
3. days
4. cities

5. sheep
6. potatoes
7. bosses

8. marches
9. mice
10. policemen

Exercise 8: Singulars

1. sky
2. fox
3. puppy
4. foot
5. fish

6. loaf
7. tooth
8. loss
9. woman
10. wish

Exercise 9

1. FEW people believe the politicians will do anything about unemployment.
2. How MUCH air is left in the tank?
3. Their baby knows MANY words for its age.
4. Taking an elephant on a trip is LITTLE trouble if you plan carefully.
5. MANY dollars add up to a lot of cash.
6. She had MANY little problems, but FEW big ones.
7. FEW problems are so difficult to solve.
8. There are too MANY cars on the road at rush hour.
9. Dora has too MANY chairs and too LITTLE other furniture.
10. MANY people would say Ron has MUCH courage.

Exercise 10

1. doctors'
2. movie's
3. Doris' or Doris's
4. boys'

5. Women's
6. bear's
7. Year's
8. weeks'

9. Lisa's, brothers'
10. Max's or Max', Joan's
11. house's
12. grandmother's
13. dollars'
14. dog's
15. Elephants', people's

ANSWERS AND EXPLANATIONS—REVIEW EXERCISE

1. The Mississippi <u>River</u> runs down to the sea. <u>River</u> is part of a proper noun, the name of a single river.

2. Only sharp <u>knives</u> cut <u>tomatoes</u> easily. Watch your plural forms.

3. <u>Many</u> accidents could be avoided. <u>Accidents</u> is a count noun.

4. Emily was tired of picking up her <u>children's</u> toys. Only plurals which already end with <u>s</u> add only an apostrophe to form the possessive.

5. In 1974 Cockburn became <u>mayor</u> of Pillburg. <u>Mayor</u> would be capitalized only if it were part of Cockburn's name, as in <u>Mayor</u> <u>Cockburn</u>.

6. The boys spent hours learning to catch <u>flies</u> with their hands. Watch your plural forms.

7. <u>Many</u> marriages end in divorce. Marriage is a count noun.

8. The federal <u>government's</u> welfare programs are not adequate.

9. <u>Matches</u> must be kept away from small children. Nouns which end in <u>sh</u>, <u>s</u>, <u>z</u>, <u>x</u>, and <u>ch</u>—**sh**ort **s**ick **z**ebras **X**-ray **ch**eaper—add <u>es</u> to form the plural.

10. What should you do when two <u>weeks'</u> pay goes in one? Two weeks must be plural; plural nouns which already end with <u>s</u> add only an apostrophe to form the possessive.

3 | VERBS

WHAT IS A VERB?

See if you can make sense of this newspaper story:

> When the fire Mr. Reyes the window and out onto the balcony. He because he he anyway. While he the railing smoke around him, people: "The firemen!"

The story makes almost no sense because the verbs have been left out. Verbs are action words. Try the story again with the verbs put back:

> When the fire broke out Mr. Reyes smashed the window and stepped out onto the balcony. He decided to jump because he thought he would die anyway. While he clutched the railing and smoke billowed around him, people shouted: "Wait! Don't jump! the firemen are coming!"

Look how many words in the story are verbs:

	to jump	
broke out	thought	shouted
smashed	would die	wait
stepped	clutched	don't jump
decided	billowed	are coming

Exercise 1

List 25 words that can finish this sentence: "I'd like to
_____." Any word that fits the sentence
will be what we call a verb.

I'd like to _____.

1. *fly*	7. _____	13. _____	19. _____
2. *dream*	8. _____	14. _____	20. _____
3. _____	9. _____	15. _____	21. _____
4. _____	10. _____	16. _____	22. _____
5. _____	11. _____	17. _____	23. _____
6. _____	12. _____	18. _____	24. _____

25. _____

Answers start on page 96.

VERB FORMS

Most verbs have five **forms.** For instance, here are the
five forms of the verb sing:

Sing!
He **sings.**
Yesterday I **sang.**
I have already **sung.**
She is **singing.**

The first of these forms is the name of the verb. The
name is the same form as the command. You can say to
someone, "please sing," but you can't say please sings, or
please sang, or please sung, or please singing.

Exercise 2

Find the first form of the verbs used below. The main verb in each sentence is underlined. Write the name of the verb in the space at right. The name of the verb is the same as the command. The first two are done as examples.

1. He's <u>drinking</u> bourbon.   *drink*

2. Susan already <u>paid</u> me five dollars.   *pay*

3. You <u>gave</u> too much.   ~~gave~~ give

4. He had never <u>shot</u> a gun before.   shot shut

5. Henry <u>drives</u> like a little old lady.   drives drive

6. <u>Quit</u> while you're ahead.   quit quit

7. She's <u>smoking</u> herself to death.   ~~smoking~~ smoke

8. The puppy <u>followed</u> John home.   ~~followed~~ follow

Check your answers before going on.

9.   I <u>cleaned</u> the table yesterday.   ~~cleaned~~ clean

10. Are you <u>speaking</u> to me?   ~~speaking~~ speak

11. How are you <u>feeling</u>?   took feel

12. Gretel <u>took</u> her son to the doctor.   ran take

13. The children <u>ran</u> home.   draws run

14. Carmen <u>draws</u> extremely well.   draw

15. Will you be <u>seeing</u> your aunt soon?   see

Answers start on page 96.

Correct your answers on this page so you can do the next exercise.

Exercise 3

Use the verbs in the last exercise to fill in this chart. Write down all five forms of the verb. Start with the name of the verb. This is the same as the command. Fill in all 15 verbs from Exercise 2. Then fill in the blank "He _drink_ ." Next fill in the blank "Yesterday I _clean_ ." Then fill in the blank "I have already _sing song_." The last form can be found by filling in the blank "She is _singing_." Many verbs have two or three forms that look alike. Don't worry if you can't figure out five different-looking forms.

Name (Command)	"He _have_	"Yesterday I _clean_	"I have already _pay_ "	"She is _pay_"
1. drink	drinks	drank	drunk	drinking
2. pay	pays	paid	paid	paying
3.				
4. _shot_				
5. _drive_				
6.				
7.				
8.				

Check your answers before going on.

9.				
10.				
11.				
12.				
13.				
14.				
15.				

Answers start on page 96.

If you had a lot of trouble with this chart, don't worry. This chapter and the next one will explain the different verb forms and when you should use them.

VERBS AND TIME

The first thing to notice about the forms of verbs is that they tell something about time. Can you see what is wrong with the following sentences?

I studied tomorrow.
I will study yesterday.
I study last week.

What's wrong is this: The verbs don't match the time of the rest of the sentences. Let's look at them one by one.

1. I studied tomorrow. When you say, "I studied," it means you studied in the past. You could correctly say: "I studied yesterday."

2. I will study yesterday. When you say, "I will study," it means you will study in the future. You could correctly say, "I will study tomorrow."

3. I study last week. When you say, "I study," you are referring to the present, or to what generally is the case. You could correctly say, "I study every night."

Exercise 4

The verbs here are underlined. In the blanks at right, state whether the verbs refer to the past, present, or future. (Present includes what is generally the case.)

1. I enjoy life.   _present_

2. Jimmy finally left his wife last week.   _past_

3. We will see him next week.   _____

4. My aunt married again at age seventy-
    two.   _____

5. I am completely broke.   _____

6. The landlord never fixes anything.   _____

7. It will cost even more next year.   _____

8. She was one of the worst liars I knew.   _____

9. The bulb burned out immediately.   _____

10. My neighbor keeps me up at night with
    music.   _____

Check your answers before going on.

11. He doesn't drink.   _____

12. I will pass the G.E.D. test sooner or later.   _____

13. She was trying to fix the handle.   _____

14. They will make up their minds when it's
    too late.   _____

15. Who told you that?   _____

16. The owner closed the store early.   _____

17. Boys that age <u>take</u> too many chances.   _____

18. We <u>had</u> a wonderful time.   _____

Answers start on page 97.

THE HE/SHE/IT S

Most verbs add an **S,** in the present, when the subject is <u>he</u>, <u>she</u>, or <u>it</u>. (Or when the subject is someone or something that could be called <u>he</u>, <u>she</u>, or <u>it</u>.)

> I **cook.**
> John **cooks.**

<u>John</u> could be called <u>he</u>, so the verb adds an **S** and becomes **cooks**. Sometimes there is a lot more to the subject. But it still could be called <u>he</u>, <u>she</u>, or <u>it</u>:

> <u>John</u> cooks. (He cooks.)
>
> <u>My</u> <u>old</u> <u>girl</u> <u>friend</u> cooks. (She cooks.)
>
> The <u>old</u> <u>man</u> <u>who</u> <u>lives</u> <u>next</u> <u>door</u> cooks. (He cooks.)

Exercise 5

Choose the correct form of the verb and write it in the blank.

1. Sherman *talks* too much. (talk, talks)
2. The years *go* slowly in prison. (go, goes)
3. Verbs _____ their subjects. (match, matches)
4. They _____ go to church. (don't, doesn't)
5. Their baby almost never _____. (cry, cries)
6. You never _____ about how I feel. (think, thinks)

7. Peter's car _____ down all the time. (break, breaks)
8. The sax player in the band _____ your cousin. (know, knows)

Check your answers before going on.

9. Last month's phone bill _____ make sense to me. (don't, doesn't)
10. The guys in the welding shop _____ to go on strike. (want, wants)
11. This new type of blade _____ you more shaves. (give, gives)
12. The potatoes _____ to cook longer. (need, needs)
13. Crying always _____ me feel better. (make, makes)
14. We _____ most of our shopping on Saturday. (do, does)
15. The dirt on the windows _____ off easily. (wipe, wipes)

Answers start on page 97.

IRREGULAR FORMS

The he/she/it **S** goes on verbs only in the present. This is the only way that most verbs change to match their subjects in the present. However, there are **three** irregular verbs which change to match their subjects in slightly more complicated ways.

1. **Have** is complicated because the he/she/it form drops a few letters.

I You They We	have	He She It	has

2. **Be** is complicated because it has a special form for I.
   Also, the he/she/it form does not look like the others.

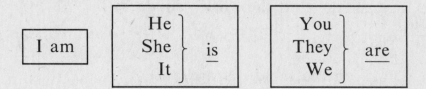

Be also has two past-forms. (Be is the ONLY verb that
changes to match its subject in the past tense.).

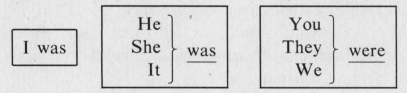

3. **Do** is complicated because the he/she/it form adds an **e**
   before the s.

I
You
They } do
We

He
She } does
It

Exercise 6

Choose the correct forms of have and be and write them in
the blanks.

1. Michael _____*is*_____ coming on the next bus.
   (is/are/am)
2. My brother _____ chin-ups with one arm.
   (do/does)
3. The children _____ tired and fell asleep.
   (was/were)
4. I _____ been awake for the last 48 hours.
   (have/has)
5. Some people _____ all the luck. (have/has)

6. She _____ look like Greta Garbo. (do/does)
7. Janet _____ engaged for two years before she got married. (was, were)
8. The best students _____ all the work. (do/does)
9. This winter _____ got to be the coldest. (has/have)
10. Your keys _____ on the table. (is/are/am)

Check your answers before going on.

11. I _____ just thinking about you. (was/were)
12. It _____ not make any difference now. (do/does)
13. We _____ more than enough time. (has/have)
14. I _____ on my way. (is/am/are)
15. The zoo _____ already closed when we arrived. (was/were)
16. Their youngest daughter _____ a limp. (has/have)
17. All our complaints _____ been ignored. (have/has)
18. _____ you really care? (Do/Does)
19. _____ your parents born in the United States? (Was/Were)
20. I _____ watching television when you called. (was/were)

Answers start on page 97.

SINGULAR AND PLURAL SUBJECTS

The he/she/it **S** is used only when the subject is singular. A **singular** subject is one person or thing. More than one person or thing is not a he, she, or it, but a they.

A subject with more than one person or thing is **plural**.

Singular	Plural
He fights.	They fight.
Grandma forgets.	Old people forget.
Today is Monday.	The days are longer.

Exercise 7

Show whether each of these subjects is singular or plural by writing S or P in the blanks.

1. My old brown shoes are missing.   *P*
2. The front bumper is rusty.   *S*
3. Getting up for work is painful.   _____
4. The whistle blows at noon.   _____
5. Some people prefer it that way.   _____
6. The rain is causing traffic to slow down.   _____
7. Have all the copies been signed?   _____
8. The eraser on this pencil is worn out.   _____

Check your answers before going on.

9. This kind of coffee tastes best.   _____
10. These are my favorite kind of candies.   _____
11. Not having a job is frightening.   _____
12. Who knows the answer?   _____
13. Tyrone loves this book.   _____
14. My children are still at school.   _____
15. The spark plugs need to be cleaned and adjusted.   _____

Answers start on page 98.

Exercise 8

Choose the correct verb forms and write them in the blanks. Remember that the <u>he/she/it</u> **S** is used on regular verbs only in the <u>present</u>. (Not all these sentences are in the present.) Irregular forms of <u>be</u> and <u>have</u> are shown on pages 82-83.

1. My socket wrenches _____were_____ stolen. (was, were)
2. The transmission _____ more work. (need, needs)
3. He will _____ by eight o'clock. (return, returns)
4. The lights _____ gone out. (have, has)
5. Running _____ good exercise. (is, are)
6. Memorizing all the verbs _____ a lot of time. (take, takes)
7. The woman next door _____ how to reach him. (know, knows)
8. The handle on this cup _____ last week. (broke, brokes)

Check your answers before going on.

9. His false teeth _____. (squeak, squeaks)
10. The men working on the house _____ two hours for lunch. (take, takes)
11. Reading newspapers _____ a good way to build your vocabulary. (is, are)
12. The shingles on the roof _____ starting to leak. (is, are)
13. They _____ a toast to winning. (drank, dranks)
14. Dogs often _____ allergies in the summer. (develop, develops)
15. High temperatures _____ food spoil. (make, makes)

Answers start on page 98.

COMPOUND SUBJECTS

Which of these sentences is correct?

John was fired.
John were fired.

The first sentence is correct. John is one person, a he. John is singular, so it takes the singular verb form was. What about this next sentence?

The men was fired.
The men were fired.

The men are more than one. The plural form were is required with the men.

Are these next examples singular or plural?

John and Steven _____ fired. (was, were)
John or Steven _____ fired. (was, were)

Subjects like John and Steven are called **compound subjects.** Here are two rules for deciding whether a compound subject is plural or singular:

1. Compound subjects with and are always plural. They never add a he/she/it S.

   The mother and her daughter look alike.

2. Compound subjects with or and nor can be either singular or plural. The verb matches the part of the subject closest to it.

   Either the boys or Ellen was responsible.
      (Ellen is closer to the verb.)
   Either Ellen or the boys were responsible.
      (The boys is closer to the verb.)

Exercise 9

Choose the correct verb forms and write them in the blanks. Compound subjects with "and" are always plural. They never add a he/she/it S. Subjects with "or" depend on which part of the subject is closest to the verb.

1. Either Margaret or her sisters ____*were*____ asking about it. (was, were)
2. France and her former colonies _____ friendly relations. (have, has)
3. Neither rain nor snow _____ the postman from his appointed rounds. (keep, keeps)
4. Saturday or Sunday _____ the best day to come. (is, are)
5. Neither cars nor airplanes _____ as safe as trains. (is, are)
6. Either glue or a few nails _____ enough to hold it. (is, are)
7. Smoking and overeating _____ a heart attack more likely. (make, makes)
8. Neither your gloves nor hat _____ in the closet. (is, are)

Check your answers before going on.

9. Either mice or birds _____ making those noises. (is, are)
10. Both Tammy and Curtis _____ garlic. (like, likes)
11. _____ the child or the parents to blame? (Is, Are)
12. The table and chairs _____ been scratched. (have, has)
13. _____ your fingers or hand burned? (Was, Were)
14. _____ her husband or children know? (Do, Does)
15. Tuesday and Wednesday _____ good for me. (is, are)

Answers start on page 98.

BY-THE-WAY INFORMATION

Is the following sentence correct?

Malcolm, like his brother, <u>is</u> over six feet tall.

The sentence is correct because the subject of the sentence is <u>Malcolm</u>. The phrase <u>like his brothers</u> is not part of the subject. It is extra information tossed in **by-the-way.** If you take it out, the sentence makes just as much sense.

Malcolm, like his brothers, is over six feet tall.
Malcolm . . . . is over six feet tall.

Here's another example. Is this one correct?

Other countries, as well as America, <u>has</u> problems.

The subject here is <u>other countries</u>. America is only <u>by-the-way</u> information, not part of the subject. The subject <u>other countries</u> is plural, so the verb should be <u>have</u> instead of <u>has</u>. Notice that the sentence makes just as much sense if you leave <u>America</u> out:

Other countries, as well as America, have problems.
Other countries . . . . have problems.

Exercise 10

Underline the by-the-way information in the following sentences. Then choose the correct verb form and write it in the blank.

1. Charlene, <u>like all the women in her family,</u> ___*has*___ a bad temper. (has, have)

2. Tooth decay, like many diseases, _____ easier to prevent than stop once started. (is, are)

3. Lyndon Johnson, more than Kennedy or Nixon, _____ responsible for the war in Vietnam. (was, were)

4. Michelle, unlike the women she works with, _____ trying to diet. (is, are)

5. Samuels, Koswalski, and Alvarez, as well as another man whose name is unknown, _____ wanted by the police. (is, are)

6. My dog, unlike most poodles, ___are___ lazy and serene. (is, are)

7. Most elm trees, unlike this one, _____ killed by Dutch elm disease. (was, were)

8. Small magazines such as this one _____ it hard to survive. (find, finds)

Check your answers before going on.

9. My friends Jack and Maxwell, but not Douglas, _____ at the mill. (works, work)

10. Love or hate, but not lack of interest, _____ a person act that way. (make, makes)

11. Tess and Laura, like their mother, _____ glasses. (wears, wear)

12. This brand, unlike all the others, _____ a two-year guarantee. (carry, carries)

13. The English language, according to many books and authors, _____ more words than any other European language. (has, have)

14. Oranges, grapefruits, and lemons, like other kinds of fruit, _____ vitamin C. (contain, contains)

15. Murder, like rape and armed robbery, _____ punished by life imprisonment in some states. (is, are)

Answers start on page 98.

TRICKY CASES: ONE OF, KIND OF

Matching the subject and verb can be tricky in certain kinds of sentences. Here are two examples. The underlined verbs are wrong.

Wrong: Pete is one of the men who <u>is</u> staying.
Wrong: They are both the kind of person who <u>make</u> me sick.

The sentences should read:

Right: Pete is one of the men who <u>are</u> staying.
Right: They are both the kind of person who <u>makes</u> me sick.

Let us look at these sentences one at a time.

1.   Pete is one of the men who are staying.

The subject of the verb <u>are</u> is <u>who</u>. <u>Who</u> is a word that stands for <u>men</u>. <u>Men</u> is plural, so the verb must be the plural form <u>are</u>. It may help you to think of the sentence this way:

Pete is one of the men. Which men?
The <u>men</u> who <u>are</u> staying.

2.   They are both the kind of person who <u>makes</u> me sick.

The subject of the verb <u>makes</u> is <u>who</u>. In this sentence, <u>who</u> stands for <u>person</u>, which is singular. You can think of this sentence in this way:

They are both the kind of person. Which person?
The <u>person</u> who <u>makes</u> me sick.

Exercise 11

Choose the correct form of the verb and write it in the blank. Find the subject of the verb by following the examples shown above.

1. There's one of the men who _____ Mr. Krankett. (know, knows)
2. He's the kind of man who _____ easily. (forgive, forgives)
3. Shelly is one of those people who _____ at everything. (laugh, laughs)
4. They bought one of those rugs that _____ on sale at Kauffman's. (was, were)
5. She is one of the greatest singers who _____ ever lived. (has, have)

Check your answers before going on.

6. Those two problems are the type that _____ me. (stump, stumps)
7. Neighborhood gossip is one of the things that _____ her. (delight, delights)
8. Isn't that one of the women who _____ at the A&P? (shop, shops)
9. Polio is one of those diseases that _____ been controlled by vaccines. (has, have)
10. They told jokes of the type that never _____ me laugh. (make, makes)

Answers start on page 99.

MORE TRICKY CASES: VERB BEFORE THE SUBJECT

In some sentences, the verb comes before the subject. This can lead to mistakes. Here is an example:

Wrong: At the end of the block <u>lives</u> three brothers.

The subject of the sentence is <u>three</u> <u>brothers</u>. <u>Three</u> <u>brothers</u> is plural. The verb should be the plural form <u>live</u>:

>   Right: At the end of the block <u>live</u> three brothers.

This kind of mistake is very common in sentences that begin with <u>there is</u> or <u>there are</u>. The subject of <u>there is</u> and <u>there are</u> always comes after them.

>   Wrong: There <u>is</u> two more beers in the refrigerator.

The subject of the sentence above is *two beers,* which is plural. The verb should be the plural form <u>are</u>. The sentence should read:

>   Right: There <u>are</u> two more beers in the refrigerator.

Exercise 12

Underline the subject in each of these sentences. Then write the correct form of the verb in the blank.

1. On top of the mountain *stand* <u>the five buildings</u>. (stand, ‘ stands)
2. There _____ a few things I want to discuss with you. (is, are)
3. Before our eyes _____ a parking lot. (was, were)
4. Out of the door _____ several girls. (run, runs)
5. There _____ a dance tonight. (is, are)

Check your answers before going on.

6. On television last night _____ two old movies. (was, were)
7. First on my list _____ butter and eggs. (is, are)

8. At the intersection of two streets _____ an old house. (stand, stands)

9. There _____ a phone book and telephone on the table. (is, are)

10. There _____ either a car or a truck in the driveway. (was, were)

Answers start on page 100.

REVIEW EXERCISE—VERBS

Each of these sentences has at least one mistake in it. Rewrite the sentences so they are correct.

1. Has all the tickets been collected?

_____

2. Both dogs and cats makes him sneeze.

_____

3. He says that either John's dogs or Mary's cat are in the room.

_____

_____

4. America is one of the countries that imports more oil than they produce.

_____

_____

5. Steve, like many people I know, love matching subjects and verbs more than anything else he does.

_____

_____

6. On either side of the border lies Brownsville and Matamoros, and the river flows between them.

_____

_____

7. There is occasional thunderstorms in the desert.

_____

8. The train to Nashville and points north don't stop here until nine o'clock.

_____

_____

9. After the storm comes peace and quiet.

_____

10. The books I told you about is due at the library.

_____

11. The dirt on the tools seem to have stained my gloves.

_____

12. Has all the newspapers been distributed?

_____

13. These eggs, in my opinion, needs more spices.

_____

14. Neither the children nor the mother have medical insurance.

_____

_____

15. Doris is one of the women who goes bowling with me.

_____

_____

ANSWERS AND EXPLANATIONS—VERBS

Exercise 1

All words that fill the blank and finish the sentence are correct.

Exercise 2

1. drink	5. drive	9. clean	13. run
2. pay	6. quit	10. speak	14. draw
3. give	7. smoke	11. feel	15. see
4. shoot	8. follow	12. take	

Exercise 3

Name (Command)	"He _____s"	"Yesterday I _____"	"I have already___"	"She is _____ing"
1. drink	drinks	drank	drunk	drinking
2. pay	pays	paid	paid	paying
3. give	gives	gave	given	giving
4. shoot	shoots	shot	shot	shooting
5. drive	drives	drove	driven	driving
6. quit	quits	quit	quit	quitting
7. smoke	smokes	smoked	smoked	smoking
8. follow	follows	followed	followed	following
9. clean	cleans	cleaned	cleaned	cleaning
10. speak	speaks	spoke	spoken	speaking
11. feel	feels	felt	felt	feeling
12. take	takes	took	taken	taking
13. run	runs	ran	run	running
14. draw	draws	drew	drawn	drawing
15. see	sees	saw	seen	seeing

Exercise 4

1. present
2. past
3. future
4. past: This sentence describes something that has already happened.
5. present: This person is broke now.
6. present: The present includes what is generally the case.
7. future
8. past
9. past
10. present: This is generally the case.
11. present: This is generally the case.
12. future: I will pass in the future.
13. past: She was trying to fix it sometime in the past.
14. future
15. past
16. past
17. present: This is generally the case.
18. past

Exercise 5

1. talks	5. cries	9. doesn't	13. makes
2. go	6. think	10. want	14. do
3. match	7. breaks	11. gives	15. wipes
4. don't	8. knows	12. need	

Exercise 6

1. is	5. have
2. does	6. does
3. were	7. was
4. have	8. do

9. has
10. are
11. was
12. does
13. have
14. am
15. was
16. has
17. have
18. Do
19. Were
20. was

Exercise 7

1. P
2. S
3. S
4. S
5. P
6. S
7. P
8. S
9. S
10. P
11. S
12. S
13. S
14. P
15. P

Exercise 8

1. were
2. needs
3. return
4. have
5. is
6. takes
7. knows
8. broke
9. squeak
10. take
11. is
12. are
13. drank
14. develop
15. make

Exercise 9

1. were
2. have
3. keeps
4. is
5. are
6. are
7. make
8. is
9. are
10. like
11. Is
12. have
13. Were
14. Does
15. are

Exercise 10

1. Charlene, like all the women in her family, **has** a bad temper.

2. Tooth decay, like many diseases, **is** easier to prevent than stop once started.

3. Lyndon Johnson, more than Kennedy or Nixon, **was** responsible for the war in Vietnam.

4. Michelle, unlike the women she works with, **is** trying to diet.

5. Samuels, Koswalski, and Alvarez, as well as another man whose name is unknown, **are** wanted by the police.

6. My dog, unlike most poodles, **is** lazy and serene.

7. Most elm trees, unlike this one, **were** killed by Dutch elm disease.

8. Small magazines such as this one **find** it hard to survive.

9. My friends Jack and Maxwell, but not Douglas, **work** at the mill.

10. Love or hate, but not lack of interest, **makes** a person act that way.

11. Tess and Laura, like their mother, **wear** glasses.

12. This brand, unlike all the others, **carries** a two-year guarantee.

13. The English language, according to many books and authors, **has** more words than any other European language.

14. Oranges, grapefruits, and lemons, like other kinds of fruit, **contain** vitamin C.

15. Murder, like rape and armed robbery, **is** punished by life imprisonment in some states.

Exercise 11

1. know
2. forgives
3. laugh
4. were
5. have

6. stumps
7. delight
8. shop
9. have
10. makes

Exercise 12

1. On top of the mountain **stand** <u>the five buildings</u>.
2. There **are** <u>a few things</u> I want to discuss with you.
3. Before our eyes **was** <u>a parking lot</u>.
4. Out of the door **run** <u>several girls</u>.
5. There **is** <u>a dance</u> tonight.
6. On television last night **were** <u>two old movies</u>.
7. First on my list **are** <u>butter and eggs</u>.
8. At the intersection of two streets **stands** <u>an old house</u>.
9. There **are** <u>a phone book and telephone</u> on the table.
10. There **was** <u>either a car or a truck</u> in the driveway.

ANSWERS AND EXPLANATIONS—REVIEW EXERCISE

1. Have all the tickets been collected?
2. Both dogs and cats make him sneeze.
3. He says that either John's dogs or Mary's cat is in the room.
4. America is one of the countries that import more oil than they produce.
5. Steve, like many people I know, loves matching subjects and verbs more than anything else he does.
6. On either side of the border lie Brownsville and Matamoros, and the river flows between them.
7. There are occasional thunderstorms in the desert.
8. The train to Nashville and points north doesn't stop here until nine o'clock.
9. After the storm come peace and quiet.
10. The books I told you about are due at the library.
11. The dirt on the tools seems to have stained my gloves.
12. Have all the newspapers been distributed?
13. These eggs, in my opinion, need more spices.
14. Neither the children nor the mother has medical insurance.
15. Doris is one of the women who go bowling with me.

4 | MORE ABOUT VERBS

AUXILIARY VERBS

Most verbs refer to either the past, present, or future.

Past: Did he drink?
Present: Does he drink?
Future: Will he drink?

In these examples the main verb is <u>drink</u>. The little verbs <u>did</u>, <u>does</u>, and <u>will</u> place the main verb in time. These little verbs are called **auxiliaries.** Auxiliaries are also called <u>helping verbs</u>.

The auxiliary <u>does</u> can be put in some sentences for emphasis.

Your mother drinks.
Never.
I've seen her. Your mother <u>does</u> drink.

In the last sentence above, <u>does</u> has been added for emphasis. Otherwise the last sentence in this conversation is the same as the first. Notice how the <u>he/she/it</u> **S** goes on <u>does</u> instead of <u>drink</u>.

Exercise 1

Here are the answers to questions. Write the questions on the lines. Follow the examples. Be sure to use the <u>he/she/it</u>

form <u>does</u> where you need to. Remember that the <u>he/she/it</u> S occurs only in the present.

1. David sings.
    Does David sing?

2. Elephants forget.
    Do elephants forget?

3. Aunt Susan knows the truth.

4. Roger will know better one day.

5. Simon walked home last week.

6. Michael means well.

7. Henry quit his job last Friday.

8. Children cry easily.

Check your answers before going on.

9. Congressman McCann said hello to the reporter.

10. Cigarette smoking stains teeth.

11. Timothy works in the hotel kitchen.

12. Luz Maria gossips too much.

13.   Gin causes the worst hangovers.

_____

14.   A strong wind blew Charlie's hat off.

_____

15.   Oak trees fall in bad storms.

_____

Answers start on page 131.

THE PAST

Most verbs have a special form for the past. In most cases, this special past-form ends with ed.

>   He lived in Nassau.
>   Carol watered our plants last week.
>   We moved to Omaha.
>   She passed me on the street.

The auxiliary in the past is did. When this auxiliary appears, the special past-form of the main verb is not used. The past-form is not necessary because the auxiliary did tells the reader that the verb is in the past.

>   He lived in Nassau.
>   He did live in Nassau.

Here is an odd fact about English: You cannot add not to a verb unless its auxiliary appears:

>   She whispered.
>   She did not whisper.

Almost all verbs have past-forms. However, not all of

these past-forms end with ed. For example, the past-form of keep is kept. The past-form of hold is held. Verbs like keep and hold are called **irregular** verbs.

> They held on.
> They did not hold on.

Observe that when the auxiliary did appears, the past-form held is not necessary. The name-form hold is used instead.

The table that follows shows almost all the irregular verbs like keep and hold. The name of the verb appears in the first column; the past-form is in the second column. We'll look at the third column later.

IRREGULAR VERBS		
Name Of Verb	**Past-Form of Verb**	**Perfect-Form of Verb**
be	was, were	been
beat	beat	beaten
become	became	become
begin	began	begun
bend	bent	bent
bet	bet	bet
bite	bit	bitten
blow	blew	blown
break	broke	broken
bring	brought	brought
build	built	built
buy	bought	bought
catch	caught	caught
choose	chose	chosen
come	came	come
cut	cut	cut
deal	dealt	dealt

IRREGULAR VERBS

Name Of Verb	Past-Form of Verb	Perfect-Form of Verb
dig	dug, digged	dug, digged
dive	dived, dove	dived
do	did	done
dream	dreamed, dreamt	dreamed, dreamt
drink	drank	drunk
drive	drove	driven
eat	ate	eaten
fall	fell	fallen
feel	felt	felt
fight	fought	fought
find	found	found
flee	fled	fled
fly	flew	flown
forget	forgot	forgotten, forgot
freeze	froze	frozen
get	got	got, gotten
give	gave	given
go	went	gone
grow	grew	grown
hang (a thing)	hung	hung
hang (a person)	hanged	hanged
have	had	had
hear	heard	heard
hold	held	held
hurt	hurt	hurt
keep	kept	kept
know	knew	known
lay (put down)	laid	laid
lead	led	led
leave	left	left
lend	lent	lent
let	let	let
lie (down)	lay	lain

IRREGULAR VERBS

Name Of Verb	Past-Form of Verb	Perfect-Form of Verb
lie (say falsely)	lied	lied
lose	lost	lost
make	made	made
meet	met	met
pay	paid	paid
prove	proved	proved, proven
put	put	put
read	read	read
ride	rode	ridden
ring	rang	rung
rise	rose	risen
run	ran	run
say	said	said
see	saw	seen
sell	sold	sold
send	sent	sent
set	set	set
shake	shook	shaken
shoot	shot	shot
show	showed	shown, showed
shrink	shrank	shrunk
sing	sang	sung
sink	sank	sunk
sit	sat	sat
sleep	slept	slept
slide	slid	slid
speak	spoke	spoken
spin	spun	spun
steal	stole	stolen
sting	stung	stung
stink	stank	stunk
strike	struck	struck
swim	swam	swum
swing	swung	swung

IRREGULAR VERBS

Name Of Verb	Past-Form of Verb	Perfect-Form of Verb
take	took	taken
teach	taught	taught
tear	tore	torn
tell	told	told
think	thought	thought
throw	threw	thrown
understand	understood	understood
wake	woke, waked	waked, woke, woken
wear	wore	worn
win	won	won
wind	wound	wound
wring	wrung	wrung
write	wrote	written

Exercise 2

The past-form of the verb should be used in all these sentences. Write the correct form in the blank. Use the table of irregular verbs if you are not sure.

1. We ___*ran*___ into him earlier. (ran/run)

2. She ___*taught*___ us a lot. (teached/taught)

3. They _____ us out of ten dollars. (cheated/chaught)

4. Marion _____ home just after twelve. (came/come)

5. The war _____ in 1914. (begun/began)

6. The cop _____ him away. (blown/blew)

7. We _____ two six-packs in half an hour. (drank/drunk)

8. They _____ asleep at once. (fell/fallen)

9. We _____ you a present. (brung/brought)

10. They _____ the shed last spring. (built/builted)

Check your answers before going on.

11. They always _____ the best of it. (made/maded)

12. We _____ at the office. (gave/given)

13. It _____ only a little. (hurt/hurted)

14. The mailman _____ him the letter. (shown/showed)

15. The bell _____ every day at noon. (rung/rang)

16. We _____ it for ourselves. (seen/saw)

17. The accident only _____ him up. (shaken/shook)

18. They _____ to me about the wedding. (spoken/spoke)

19. I _____ what I was saying. (forgot/forgotten)

20. The ship _____ in minutes. (sank/sunk)

Answers start on page 131.

Test yourself to see which of the irregular past-forms you need to study. Use the table of irregular verbs. Cover the first and second columns with two strips of paper. Pull down the first strip of paper to show the name of the first verb. Try to think of the correct past-form which is hidden by the second strip of paper. To help think of the correct form, imagine what word would go in this sentence:

I _____ yesterday.

Once you have decided what you think the past-form should be, pull the second strip of paper down and see if you are right. If you are right, go on to the next verb. If you are wrong, make a mark next to the past-form.

When you are through with the list, all the past-forms you don't know will be marked. Study these. On a separate piece of paper, practice these past-forms by writing sentences that use them. Write a different sentence for each one.

ASPECT

A man and a woman were sitting in a doctor's waiting room. They were alone. The man took out a pack of cigarettes and put one in his mouth.

"Are you smoking?" he asked the woman.

"I beg your pardon?" she replied.

"Are you smoking?" he repeated.

She looked at him as if he were crazy. "Of course I'm not smoking," she said. "You can see that I'm not smoking."

"But are you smoking?" asked the man a third time, waving his cigarettes at her.

The woman got up and left the room.

Was the man crazy? No; he only made a mistake in **aspect**. Aspect tells such things as whether an action is finished and whether it is done often.

What the man meant to ask was, "Do you smoke?" He

wanted to offer the woman a cigarette. What he said instead was, "Are you smoking?" Both these questions are in the present, but they have different aspects. The first question means right now, but the second question means as a habit.

There are four aspects in all. Here is how they look when used in the present:

Simple: I smoke. (Or: I do smoke)
-ing: I am smoking.
Perfect: I have smoked.
-ing perfect: I have been smoking.

These four aspects can each be used in the past and future as well as in the present. There are twelve combinations in all. All twelve are shown on the chart *12 Ways That Verbs Are Used*. This chart uses the verb speak and the subject I as an example.

12 WAYS THAT VERBS ARE USED			
	Past	Present	Future
Simple Aspect	I did speak. (Or: I spoke)	I do speak. (Or: I speak)	I will speak.
-ing Aspect	I was speaking.	I am speaking.	I will be speaking.
Perfect Aspect	I had spoken.	I have spoken.	I will have spoken.
-ing Perfect Aspect	I had been speaking.	I have been speaking.	I will have been speaking.

Exercise 3

Look back at the chart *12 Ways That Verbs Are Used*. Make a chart like it using this blank chart. Use the verb drink instead of speak. The forms of drink were shown in Exercise 3, chapter 3, page 78.

12 WAYS THAT VERBS ARE USED			
Simple Aspect			
Ing Aspect			
Perfect Aspect			
Ing-Perfect Aspect			

Answers start on page 132.

THE ING ASPECT

The **ing aspect** can be used in the past, the present, and the future.

Past -ing: I was speaking.
Present -ing: I am speaking.
Future -ing: I will be speaking.

The ing aspect gets its name from the fact that the main verb always adds ing. There are no exceptions.

I was joking.
He is being good.
They will be leaving at dawn.

The auxiliary of the ing aspect is always a form of **be**. The auxiliary of the past ing is **was** or **were**, the past-forms of **be**. The auxiliary of the present ing is **am**, **is**, or **are**, the present-forms of **be**. The auxiliary of the future ing is **will be**, the future-form of **be**.

If you are not sure how to use the different forms of be, refer back to the Do, Have, Be section in chapter 3.

The main problems that people have with the ing aspect are:

1. Using the wrong form of the auxiliary be.

   They was lying.
   (Should be: They were lying.)

2. Not using any auxiliary at all.

   I tell you, man, they lying.
   (Should be: they were lying, or are lying.)

Exercise 4

All these sentences are in the simple present. Rewrite them in the ing present using am, is, or are as the auxiliary.

1. She plays the flute beautifully.
   She is playing the flute beautifully.

2. Do they travel by car?
   Are they traveling by car?

3. Mathilde keeps her phone book in the dresser.

4.   I make up my mind.

_____

5.   My grandfather's legs hurt him today.

_____

Check your answers before going on.

    Now let's try some in the past. Your auxiliary must now be one of two past-forms of be: was or were. The first sentence is done as an example.

6.   He talked in class.
     He was talking in class.

7.   He drove very fast.

_____

8.   Did they have a good time?

_____

9.   Mabel and Oliver went out together for a year.

_____

10.   Maureen thought of a better answer.

_____

Check your answers before going on.

    Now try some in the future. Your auxiliary must be the future-form of be: will be.

11.   Cynthia will arrive tomorrow morning.

_____

12.   They will cry at the end.

_____

13.   The plane will land at San Juan.

_____

14.   I will make more money next year.

_____

15.   She will regret this forever.

_____

Answers start on page 132.

THE PERFECT ASPECT

The third aspect is the **perfect aspect.** Here are examples of the perfect aspect used in the past, present, and future:

Past Perfect: She had taken.
Present Perfect: She has taken.
Future Perfect: She will have taken.

The auxiliary for the perfect aspect is always a form of the verb have: had for the past perfect, have or has for the present perfect, and will have for the future perfect.

For the main verb, a special form called the perfect-form is used:

I have taken.
I have gone.
I have been.

Taken is the perfect-form of take; **gone** is the perfect-form of go; **been** is the perfect form of be. These three verbs are irregular. Other irregular perfect-forms are shown in column three of the table of irregular verbs (pages 104-107).

Exercise 5

Write answers to these questions. Use the present perfect, as shown in the examples. All the verbs are irregular. You will find the correct perfect-forms to be used in the table of irregular verbs (pages 104-107). Your auxiliary must be one of the present forms of have (have or has).

1. Are you giving up?
    I have given up already.

2. Will the sweater shrink in hot water?
    It has shrunk already.

3. Will you take him to the zoo?

4. Will you throw me the ball?

5. How soon will the tires wear out?

Check your answers before going on.

6. Are you going to write to your mother?

7. Will Jonathan speak to his brother?

8. Will someone steal the money?

9. Can Matthew swim across the English Channel?

10. Is Henry going to Detroit?

Check your answers before going on.

11. Did they choose a name for the baby?

_____

12. Will snow fall?

_____

13. Will Sugar Ray win the fight?

_____

14. Is Pamela doing the crossword puzzle?

_____

15. Are you selling your car?

_____

Answers start on page 133.

THE DIFFERENCE BETWEEN THE PERFECT AND THE SIMPLE PAST

All the questions in the last exercise used irregular verbs. That's why you had to look up their perfect-forms on the table of irregular verbs. The perfect-forms of most verbs, however, are just like their past-forms:

past-form	perfect-form

I walked.   I have walked.
He laughed.   He has laughed.
She turned.   She has turned.

The perfect-forms and past-forms of many irregular verbs, however, are different:

I went.   I have gone.

Since the past-forms and perfect-forms are the same in so many verbs, people make the mistake of thinking they are always the same. They write things like:

> MISTAKE: I <u>have went</u>.

The way to prevent this sort of mistake is to study the perfect-forms of all the irregular verbs. These are shown in column three of the table of irregular verbs (pages 104-107). You must use these perfect-forms when the auxiliary is <u>have</u>, <u>has</u>, or <u>had</u>.

Test yourself to see which of the irregular perfect-forms you need to study. Do this the same way you tested yourself on the <u>past</u>-forms. Mark all the perfect-forms that you don't know. Then write sentences using each of these perfect-forms.

Exercise 6

In this exercise, you have to decide whether the past-form or perfect-form is correct. Write the correct form in the blank. Look back to the table of irregular verbs (pages 104-107) when you need to. Remember that the perfect-form is used with the auxiliaries <u>have</u>, <u>has</u>, or <u>had</u>. The past-form is used alone.

1. They say he has _____ over one thousand cars. (stole/stolen)

2. She _____ upstairs when the baby cried. (ran/run)

3. Have you _____ a letter lately? (wrote/written)

4. He has _____ too many chances. (took/taken)

5.   Who _____ it? (done/did)

6.   Who has _____ it? (done/did)

7.   The Indians had _____ to America long before Columbus. (came/come)

8.   If you had _____ him a map he wouldn't be lost. (drew/drawn)

9.   They _____ away the tickets by mistake. (threw/thrown)

10. We have _____ to him several times. (spoke/spoken)

Check your answers before going on.

11. He _____ underwater. (swam/swum)

12. Have you _____ the bell? (rang/rung)

13. The pigeon _____ out of reach. (flew/flown)

14. Has the ice _____ yet? (froze/frozen)

15. They have _____ us at our own game. (beat/beaten)

16. The weather has _____ cooler. (became/become)

17. Has Arthur _____ to the movies? (went/gone)

18. I said hello and he _____ up at me. (blew/blown)

19. This bird has _____. (flew/flown)

20. They had _____ all about us. (forgot/forgotten)

Answers start on page 133.

MAKING YOUR ENGLISH STANDARD:
DONE SAID, GONE SAID, DONE GONE SAID

The following expressions are common in many parts of the United States.

> He done said.
> He gone said.
> He done gone said.

These forms are not part of what is called Standard English. Standard English is the version of English that most tests are based on. For this reason, "he done said" is considered wrong.

How can you translate these expressions into Standard English? One way is to replace done, gone, or done gone with a form of have:

Everyday English	Standard English (Present Perfect)
He done told me.	He has told me.

The trouble is that these two expressions don't mean exactly the same thing. It might be better to translate "he done told me" in some other way:

Everyday English	Standard English
He done told me.	He did tell me.
	He told me.
	He had told me.
	He has told me.

All the expressions at right are possible translations for "he done told me." You have to decide yourself which one sounds best in any given case.

Rewrite these sentences so they are in Standard English. You will have to decide which translation sounds best. Check your answers with a friend.

1.   You done told me the story already.

_____

2.   He gone left his wife for another woman.

_____

3.   Before I could ask, he done give me the answer.

_____

4.   I done gone helped you out for the last time.

_____

5.   Kathleen and John done got married last week.

_____

CONTRACTIONS

People like to run their words together. Instead of saying "I do not," they say, "I don't." This is perfectly correct. These run-together words are called **contractions.**

$$do + not = don't$$
$$has + not = hasn't$$
$$does + not = doesn't$$

As you can see, the O in <u>not</u> gets left out. The **apostrophe** (') marks the place of the missing O. Sometimes other letters are left out:

it + has = it's
can + not = can't
they + are = they're

One contraction is irregular:

will + not = won't

Exercise 7

Write in the correct contraction in the blanks. Be sure to correct your answers with the answer key for this exercise, so you'll have a list to study.

1. do + not   =_____

2. has + not   =_____

3. does + not   =_____

4. is + not   =_____

5. are + not   =_____

6. will + not   =_____

7. did + not   =_____

8. have + not   =_____

9. was + not   =_____

10. were + not   =_____

11. can + not   =_____

12. could + not   =_____

13. would + not   =_____

14. should + not   =_____

15. I + am   =_____

16. he + is   =_____

17. you + are   =_____

18. we + are   =_____

19. they + are   =_____

20. I + have   =_____

21. you + have   =_____

22. he + has   =_____

23. she + has   =_____

24. it + has   =_____

25. we + have   =_____

26. they + have   =_____

27. who + is   =_____

28. let + us   =_____

29. Jane + is   =_____

30. someone + is   =_____

Answers start on page 134.

MAKING YOUR ENGLISH STANDARD: AIN'T

Ain't is a very common word, but it is not part of
Standard English. Ain't stands for Standard English am
not, is not, are not, have not, has not. These Standard
expressions are usually used as contractions. For instance:

Everyday English	Standard English

He ain't here.	He is not here.
	(Contractions:
	    He isn't here.
	    He's not here.)

I ain't sick.	I am not sick. (Contraction: I'm not sick.)

Exercise 8

Rewrite these sentences so they are in Standard English.

1. She ain't sick.
   She is not sick. (or: *She isn't sick.* or: *She's not sick.*)

2. They ain't here.
   They are not here. (or: *They aren't here.* or: *They're not here.*)

3. It ain't green.

4. They ain't rich.

5. You ain't the one.

6. I ain't his friend.

Check your answers before going on.

7.   I ain't afraid.

_____

8.   He ain't so smart.

_____

9.   You ain't so bad.

_____

10.   We ain't drunk.

_____

11.   Ain't they ugly?

_____

12.   Ain't you something?

_____

Answers start on page 134.

When ain't is the auxiliary of a verb, it can mean one of two things. It can mean a form of be not (am not, is not, are not), or it can mean a form of have not (have not, has not).

Everyday English	Standard English
You ain't listening.	You are not listening.
You ain't listened.	You have not listened.

When the verb ends with ing (listening), the auxiliary is a form of be (am, is, are). When the verb is a past participle like listened, however, the auxiliary is a form of have (have, has). Here are all the possibilities:

	Everyday English	Standard English
-ing Form	I ain't listening.	I <u>am</u> <u>not</u> listening.
	He She ain't listening. It	He She <u>is</u> <u>not</u> listening. It
	You We ain't listening. They	You We <u>are</u> <u>not</u> listening. They
Past Participle	I ain't listened.	I <u>have</u> <u>not</u> listened.
	He She ain't listened. It	He She <u>has</u> not listened. It
	You We ain't listened. They	You We <u>have</u> <u>not</u> listened. They

Standard contractions are not shown here because they would make things seem very complicated. (For instance, <u>he</u> <u>is</u> <u>not</u> can also be <u>he's</u> <u>not</u> and <u>he</u> <u>isn't</u>.)

Exercise 9

Use the information above to translate these everyday sentences into Standard English. First decide whether the verb is an <u>ing</u>-form or a past participle. This will tell you whether to use a form of <u>be</u> (<u>am</u>, <u>is</u>, <u>are</u>) or a form of <u>have</u> (<u>have</u> or <u>has</u>). Then look at the subject of the sentence (<u>I</u>, <u>you</u>, <u>she</u>, and so forth) to see which form of <u>be</u> or <u>have</u> you should use.

1. You ain't listened.
   You have not listened (or: *You haven't listened.*)

2. Mary ain't talking.
   Mary is not talking. (or: *Mary isn't talking.* or: *Mary's not talking.*)

3. They ain't helping themselves.

4. Sam ain't going to be there.

5. I ain't told you the best part.

6. You ain't got a chance.

Check your answers before going on.

7. You ain't fooling me.

8. She ain't gone to bed yet.

9. They ain't still living there.

10. Clyde and Marsha ain't feeling any better.

11. We ain't seen him since Monday.

12. The roof ain't got a leak.

Answers start on page 135.

REVIEW EXERCISE—MORE ABOUT VERBS

This exercise gives you more practice. It will review much of what you learned in this chapter. Read each sentence. The underlined word or words may be wrong. Choose the BEST answer from those given. Place a check (✔) next to it in the space. If there is nothing wrong with the sentence check 5 no change.

1. When I came to Chicago in 1958, I will have only ten dollars.

  _____(1) had

  _____(2) would have

  _____(3) has

  _____(4) got

  _____(5) no change

2. Republican leaders say the bills was too costly.

  _____(1) ain't

  _____(2) is

  _____(3) be

  _____(4) were

  _____(5) no change

3. Democratic politicians insist that ain't so.

  _____(1) aren't

  _____(2) are not

  _____(3) is not

  _____(4) were not

  _____(5) no change

4.   I took the one less traveled by.

_____(1) have took

_____(2) taken

_____(3) had took

_____(4) has taken

_____(5) no change

5.   She done everything that she possibly could.

_____(1) doing

_____(2) have did

_____(3) has did

_____(4) did

_____(5) no change

6.   They drank and sung songs late into the night.

_____(1) drank and sang

_____(2) drunk and sung

_____(3) drinked and sung

_____(4) have drank and sung

_____(5) no change

7.   They were there an hour before we arrived.

_____(1) was

_____(2) been

_____(3) is

_____(4) be

_____(5) no change

8. Jacob <u>don't know</u> the full story.

_____(1) know

_____(2) doesn't know

_____(3) do know

_____(4) do not know

_____(5) no change

9. I thought he got lost, and all the time he <u>waiting</u> at another restaurant.

_____(1) been waiting

_____(2) is waiting

_____(3) was waiting

_____(4) were waiting

_____(5) no change

10. We <u>ain't seen</u> her since she came back from Tennessee.

_____(1) haven't seen

_____(2) hasn't seen

_____(3) haven't saw

_____(4) hasn't saw

_____(5) no change

11. If you <u>had drawn</u> him a map he wouldn't be lost.

_____(1) had drew

_____(2) had drawed

_____(3) drawn

_____(4) drawed

_____(5) no change

12. He <u>done left</u> his wife and took the train to Cleveland.

_____(1) left

_____(2) have left

_____(3) done gone and left

_____(4) leave

_____(5) no change

13. They say that <u>your</u> the one who's making all the trouble.

_____(1) you's

_____(2) you

_____(3) you're

_____(4) you was

_____(5) no change

14. You <u>ain't heard</u> a single word I said.

_____(1) hasn't heard

_____(2) haven't heard

_____(3) haven't heared

_____(4) hasn't heared

_____(5) no change

15. That store <u>don't got</u> what I'm looking for.

_____(1) hasn't got

_____(2) haven't got

_____(3) doesn't got

_____(4) didn't got

_____(5) no change

ANSWERS AND EXPLANATIONS—MORE ABOUT VERBS

Exercise 1

1. Does David sing?
2. Do elephants forget?
3. Does Aunt Susan know the truth?
4. Will Roger know better one day?
5. Did Simon walk home last week?
6. Does Michael mean well?
7. Did Henry quit his job last Friday?
8. Do children cry easily?

9. Did Congressman McCann say hello to the reporter?
10. Does cigarette smoking stain teeth?
11. Does Timothy work in the hotel kitchen?
12. Does Luz Maria gossip too much?
13. Does gin cause the worst hangovers?
14. Did a strong wind blow Charlie's hat off?
15. Do oak trees fall in bad storms?

Exercise 2

1. ran
2. taught
3. cheated
4. came
5. began
6. blew
7. drank
8. fell
9. brought
10. built
11. made
12. gave
13. hurt
14. showed
15. rang
16. saw
17. shook
18. spoke
19. forgot
20. sank

Exercise 3

12 WAYS THAT VERBS ARE USED			
	Past	**Present**	**Future**
Simple Aspect	I did drink. (Or: I drank)	I do drink. (Or: I drink)	I will drink.
-ing Aspect	I was drinking.	I am drinking.	I will be drinking.
Perfect Aspect	I had drunk.	I have drunk.	I will have drunk.
-ing Perfect Aspect	I had been drinking.	I have been drinking.	I will have been drinking.

Exercise 4

1. She is playing the flute beautifully.
2. Are they traveling by car?
3. Mathilde is keeping her phone book in the dresser.
4. I am making up my mind.
5. My grandfather's legs are hurting him today.

6. He was talking in class.
7. He was driving very fast.
8. Were they having a good time?
9. Mabel and Oliver were going out together for a year.
10. Maureen was thinking of a better answer.

11. Cynthia will be arriving tomorrow morning.
12. They will be crying at the end.

13. The plane will be landing at San Juan.
14. I will be making more money next year.
15. She will be regretting this forever.

Exercise 5

1. I have given up already.
2. It has shrunk already.
3. I have taken him to the zoo already.
4. I have thrown you the ball already.
5. The tires have worn out already.

6. I have written to my mother already.
7. Jonathan has spoken to his brother already.
8. Someone has stolen the money already.
9. Matthew has swum across the English Channel already.
10. Henry has gone to Detroit already.

11. They have chosen a name for the baby already.
12. Snow has fallen already.
13. Sugar Ray has won the fight already.
14. Pamela has done the crossword puzzle already.
15. I have sold my car already.

Exercise 6

1.	stolen	11.	swam
2.	ran	12.	rung
3.	written	13.	flew
4.	taken	14.	frozen
5.	did	15.	beaten
6.	done	16.	become
7.	come	17.	gone
8.	drawn	18.	blew
9.	threw	19.	flown
10.	spoken	20.	forgotten

Exercise 7

1.	don't	16.	he's
2.	hasn't	17.	you're
3.	doesn't	18.	we're
4.	isn't	19.	they're
5.	aren't	20.	I've
6.	won't	21.	you've
7.	didn't	22.	he's
8.	haven't	23.	she's
9.	wasn't	24.	it's
10.	weren't	25.	we've
11.	can't	26.	they've
12.	couldn't	27.	who's
13.	wouldn't	28.	let's
14.	shouldn't	29.	Jane's
15.	I'm	30.	someone's

Exercise 8

1. She is not sick. (She isn't sick. She's not sick.)
2. They are not here. (They're not here. They aren't here.)
3. It is not green. (It isn't green. It's not green.)
4. They are not rich. (They're not rich. They aren't rich.)
5. You are not the one. (You aren't the one. You're not the one.)
6. I am not his friend. (I'm not his friend.)

7. I am not afraid. (I'm not afraid.)
8. He is not so smart. (He isn't so smart. He's not so smart.)
9. You are not so bad. (You aren't so bad. You're not so bad.)
10. We are not drunk. (We're not drunk. We aren't drunk.)
11. Aren't they ugly? (Are they not ugly?)
12. Aren't you something? (Are you not something?)

Exercise 9

1. You have not listened. (You haven't listened.)
2. Mary is not talking. (Mary's not talking. Mary isn't talking.)
3. They are not helping themselves. (They're not helping themselves. They aren't helping themselves.)
4. Sam is not going to be there. (Sam's not going to be there. Sam isn't going to be there.)
5. I have not told you the best part. (I haven't told you the best part.)
6. You have not got a chance. (You haven't got a chance.)

7. You are not fooling me. (You aren't fooling me. You're not fooling me.)
8. She has not gone to bed yet. (She hasn't gone to bed yet.)
9. They are not still living there. (They're not still living there. They aren't still living there.)
10. Clyde and Marsha are not feeling any better. (Clyde and Marsha aren't feeling any better.)
11. We have not seen him since Monday. (We haven't seen him since Monday.)
12. The roof has not got a leak. (The roof hasn't got a leak.)

ANSWERS AND EXPLANATIONS—REVIEW EXERCISE

1. (1) When I came to Chicago in 1958, I <u>had</u> only ten dollars.
2. (4) Republican leaders say the bills <u>were</u> too costly.
3. (3) Democratic politicians insist that <u>isn't</u> so.
4. (5) No change. I <u>took</u> the one less traveled by.
5. (4) She <u>did</u> everything that she possibly could.
6. (1) They <u>drank and sang</u> songs late into the night.

7. (5) No change. They <u>were</u> there an hour before we arrived.

8. (2) Jacob <u>doesn't know</u> the full story.

9. (3) I thought he got lost, and all the time he <u>was waiting</u> at another restaurant.

10. (1) We <u>haven't seen</u> her since she came back from Tennessee.

11. (5) No change. If you <u>had drawn</u> him a map he wouldn't be lost.

12. (1) He <u>left</u> his wife and took the train to Cleveland.

13. (3) They say that <u>you're</u> the one who's making all the trouble.

14. (2) You <u>haven't heard</u> a single word I said.

15. (1) That store <u>hasn't got</u> what I'm looking for.

5 PRONOUNS

WHAT IS A PRONOUN?

People who write papers for use in court trials must use very exact language. Such a person might write:

> Mr. Phidias Dortch burned the premises at
> 27 Pine Street.

Someone who is not so exact might write in more general terms:

> The man burned the house.

If you wanted to put it as generally as possible, you might write:

> He burned it.

He and it are almost as general as you can get. He and it are called pronouns. **Pronouns** are words which take the place of nouns.

Why would you want to use pronouns if they are so general and vague? Suppose you have many things to say about Mr. Dortch:

> Mr. Dortch burned the premises at 27 Pine Street. Then Mr. Dortch got into Mr. Dortch's car and drove to Mr. Dortch's home, where Mr. Dortch washed Mr. Dortch's hands and hid in the cellar.

This would be easier to read if we take out some of the Mr. Dortch's and put pronouns in their places.

> Mr. Dortch burned the premises at 27 Pine Street. Then he got into his car and drove to his home, where he washed his hands and hid in the cellar.

The second version is just as exact as the first. We know that he and his stand for Mr. Dortch and Mr. Dortch's. Mr. Dortch is the antecedent of the pronouns he and his. The **antecedent** of a pronoun is the word or words which tell you what the pronoun stands for.

Example: Jane washed her hair.

Jane is the antecedent of her; the sentence means:

> Jane washed Jane's hair.

Exercise 1

Some pronouns are underlined in these sentences. Draw a circle around the antecedents of the underlined pronouns. Ask yourself who or what the pronouns stand for. The first one has been done as an example.

1. (Jack) thinks he is a lady-killer.
2. My cousins send their love.
3. Ellen knows she is sick.
4. Bob and Betty changed their minds.
5. The government should mind its own business.
6. Carol says she can't come.
7. Kelly's brother lost his glove.
8. When did Bob's nephew quit his job?

Check your answers before going on.

9. Nancy told her daughter she could have <u>her</u> old bracelet.

10. She put the letter back in <u>its</u> envelope.

11. Midge helped Nel wash <u>her</u> hair.

12. Joey has the flu, but there's nothing we can do about <u>it</u>.

13. Whatever Sam told Phil made him angry, for <u>he</u> turned and scowled.

14. Evil is <u>its</u> own punishment.

15. Since <u>she</u> left home, Drusilla has been happier.

Answers start on page 159.

You need to know about antecedents in order to avoid a common error. People often write sentences in which the reader can't tell what the pronouns stand for. For example:

Mary's youngest daughter was married when she was thirty-seven years old.

When <u>who</u> was thirty-seven years old? The way the sentence is written, it could mean:

Mary's youngest daughter was married when <u>the</u> <u>daughter</u> was thirty-seven years old.

The reason the sentence takes on this meaning is that pronouns always seem to stand for the <u>nearest</u> noun, which in this case is <u>daughter</u>. However, the writer meant that Mary was 37 years old. To make clear that <u>she</u> means <u>Mary</u>, the sentence must be changed:

When Mary was thirty-seven years old, her
youngest daughter was married.

or

Her youngest daughter was married when
Mary was thirty-seven years old.

Here's another example:

Helen tapped Susan's shoulder from behind
and held her breath.

Held <u>whose</u> breath? Helen held her <u>own</u> breath, but the
sentence makes it seem that Helen held Susan's breath.
Since this is impossible the sentence should be made clear.

Helen held <u>her</u> breath and tapped Susan's
shoulder from behind.

or

After tapping Susan's shoulder from behind,
Helen held her breath.

Exercise 2

Rewrite the following sentences on the lines so that it is clear
who or what the pronouns belong to.

1. When Steve's friend knocked on the door he was in the
    shower.
    Steve was in the shower when his friend knocked on
    the door.

2. When Craig's father remarried he was only seven years
    old.

3. The man shook Hank's hand and told him his name was Paul.

_____

4. By the time Mrs. Peabody's daughter was married, she was dead.

_____

5. William's father died just before he was born.

_____

Answers start on page 159.

CASE

Nouns can be both subjects and objects. Let's take two nouns, John and Jane, and let them take turns being the subject and object of a sentence.

1. John loves Jane.
2. Jane loves John.

In the first sentence, John does the loving and Jane is loved; John is the subject and Jane the object. In the second sentence, the lucky couple's roles are reversed. The only difference between the two sentences is the order of the words.

If we replace John and Jane with pronouns we get:

1. He loves her.
2. She loves him.

What happened? In the first pair of sentences John was John whether he was the subject or object, but when we switch to pronouns we get two different words, he and him. Jane was Jane whether she loved or was loved, but with pronouns we have she and her.

Here is what is going on: English uses different pronouns to show who is the subject and who is the object. You may have thought subjects and objects were something new to you, but you've really known the difference as long as you've spoken English. You show that you know the difference every time you choose between the two kinds of pronouns.

Subject Pronouns	Object Pronouns
I	me
you	you
he	him
she	her
it	it
we	us
they	them

Note: It and you have only one form for both subject and object.

Exercise 3

A subject pronoun and an object pronoun are shown at the end of each sentence. Write the correct pronoun in the blank. The first one has been done.

1. _____He_____ has a pretty good job. (He/Him)

2. They told _____ to come back later. (we/us)

3. I know I didn't tell _____. (they/them)

4. Anne visited _____ last week. (we/us)

5. Bill warned _____ of the problem. (she/her)

6. _____ have always liked movies, but _____ are getting so expensive. (We/Us) (they/them)

7. Barry loaned his socket wrenches to _____. (them/they)

8. _____ enjoyed seeing you very much. (I/Me)

Check your answers before going on.

9. Did _____ catch any fish? (he/him)

10. This will make _____ laugh. (she/her)

11. I hope _____ won't forget. (they/them)

12. Who taught _____ to play chess? (she/her)

13. You aren't taking _____ seriously. (they/them)

14. I don't think these boots will fit _____. (him/he)

15. _____ has always talked that way. (She/Her)

Answers start on page 159.

COMPOUND SUBJECTS AND OBJECTS

What is the subject of the following sentence?

My uncle, my aunt, and my cousins came to visit last Sunday.

The subject is: <u>my</u> <u>uncle</u>, <u>my</u> <u>aunt</u>, <u>and</u> <u>my</u> <u>cousins</u>. This is called a **compound subject** because it has more than one noun. If the nouns are replaced by pronouns, <u>all</u> the pronouns must be subject pronouns:

<u>He</u>, <u>she</u>, and <u>they</u> came to visit last Sunday.

There are also compound <u>objects</u>, where the object contains several nouns or pronouns.

We visited my uncle, my aunt, and my cousins.

Here the pronouns must all be object pronouns:

We visited <u>him</u>, <u>her</u>, and <u>them</u>.

Exercise 4

Fill in the blank with the right pronoun.

1. Brad and _____ fight all the time. (me, I)

2. Can you see Tony and _____? (her, she)

3. Selma and _____ are good friends. (he, him)

4. I gave it to Lisa and _____. (them, they)

5. Joe and _____ play poker every Wednesday. (he, him)

6. We found Sherman and _____ over on Broadway. (they, them)

7. Greg and _____ get along pretty well. (me, I)

8. They asked my husband and _____ to visit them.
    (me, I)

9. Mark brought Sharon and _____ to the museum.
    (he, him)

10. The difference between you and _____ is that we
    have been there before. (us, we)

Answers start on page 160.

OBJECTS OF PREPOSITIONS

Object pronouns are always used after prepositions.
Prepositions are words like <u>over</u>, <u>under</u>, <u>around</u>, and
<u>through</u>.

She walks all over him.

This doesn't seem too hard, does it? No one would write:

MISTAKE: She walks all over <u>he</u>.

But sometimes there are several objects after a preposition, and by the time the writer gets to the last one he forgets
it should be an object.

MISTAKE: She walks all over John, Calvin,
            Rupert, Marvin, Jake, Sydney,
            and <u>he</u>.

This mistake often happens with the preposition
<u>between</u>, because <u>between</u> often has two objects after it.

WRONG: We divided it between John and
          I.

RIGHT: We divided it between John and
          me.

The second sentence above is the correct one. <u>Between</u> is a preposition, and any pronoun which comes after it must be an object pronoun.

Sometimes the pronouns are separated from the prepositions by other words, but they are still objects:

WRONG: The bride's relatives threw rice
          over everyone, especially <u>she</u>.

RIGHT: The bride's relatives threw rice
          over everyone, especially <u>her</u>.

Exercise 5

Prepositions are used in these sentences. Some of the pronouns that follow them are wrong. They should all be object pronouns. Use the chart of subject and object pronouns on page 142. If the pronouns are wrong, write the correct pronouns in the blanks at right. If they are already correct, write "correct." The first one has been done as an example.

1. The birds flew over Sally and <u>he</u>.   *him*

2. A fight broke out between the boys from
   Carteret and <u>we</u>.   _____

3. I've been around Mary and <u>he</u> long enough
   to expect such things from <u>them</u>.   _____

4. I'm afraid the child will come between my
   wife and <u>I</u>.   _____

5. Luckily the bullet passed over everyone, including <u>they</u>.

_____

6. Strange things happen around Peggy and <u>she</u>.

_____

7. This was a present from John's wife, her sister, and <u>him</u>.

_____

8. Mr. Traskos left with his wife, her brother, and <u>they</u>.

_____

Check your answers before going on.

9. This was delivered to Aaron and <u>her</u> at home.

_____

10. The card was for Jim as well as <u>I</u>.

_____

11. A look of astonishment came over Carla's brother and <u>her</u>.

_____

12. They sat down next to Bobby and <u>I</u>.

_____

13. She prefers to travel without her husband or <u>you</u>.

_____

14. It is all because of Judy and <u>he</u>.

_____

15. This dinner was made possible by Curtis, Carter, and <u>I</u>.

_____

Answers start on page 160.

POSSESSIVE PRONOUNS

Consider the following sentence:

Jane's problems are Jane's.

<u>Jane's</u> is the possessive form of <u>Jane</u>. It shows that something belongs to Jane.

If we put pronouns in place of the nouns, we get:

Her problems are hers.

In the first sentence we had the word Jane's twice, but in the second sentence we get the words her and hers. Can you figure out why? Her and hers are **possessive pronouns.** Possessive pronouns take the place of words like Jane's.

English has two sets of possessive pronouns. One set is used in front of a noun:

her problem

your glasses

our idea

The other set is used alone:

her problem is hers

your glasses are yours

our idea is ours

TABLE OF POSSESSIVE PRONOUNS	
Used Before a Noun	Used Alone
my	mine
your	yours
his	his
her	hers
its	its
our	ours
their	theirs

Note that <u>its</u> and <u>his</u> have only one form. Note also that none of the possessive pronouns has an apostrophe. Don't confuse the possessive pronoun <u>its</u> (without an apostrophe) with the contraction <u>it's</u>. <u>It's</u> means <u>it is</u>. Don't confuse the possessive pronoun <u>your</u> (without an apostrophe) with the contraction <u>you're</u>. <u>You're</u> means <u>you are</u>.

Exercise 6

In the space write the correct word for each of the following sentences. The first one has been done as an example.

1. The dog chased *its* tail. (its/it's)

2. Your children are older than _____. (their/theirs)

3. We don't feel like it's really _____. (our/ours.)

4. _____ name is Indonesian. (My/Mine)

5. He ate _____ sandwich. (your/you're)

6. The car is _____ only till the bank tracks them down. (their/theirs)

7. _____ a shame, if you ask me. (Its/It's)

8. This is _____ problem. (they're/their)

Check your answers before going on.

9. Their children are older than _____. (our/ours)

10. Here's yours. Have you seen _____? (my/mine)

11.   You left _____ keys on the table. (your/you're)

12.   Ask the Peytons who _____ doctor is. (they're/their)

13.   I'd like to find earrings like _____. (her/hers)

14.   The boat pulled loose from _____ moorings. (its/it's)

15.   I think _____ still in California. (they're/their)

Answers start on page 160.

NUMBER

Like nouns, pronouns are singular and plural. For instance, the pronoun <u>he</u> means one person. The pronoun <u>they</u> means two or more. This gives us sentences like:

He is here.
They are here.

<u>Is</u> goes with singular subjects, <u>are</u> with plural subjects.

There are pronouns in English which <u>seem</u> to be plural because they refer to groups of people. These are special. They take singular verbs. The pronoun <u>everyone</u> is such a word:

RIGHT: Everyone <u>is</u> here.

WRONG: Everyone are here.

Because <u>everyone</u> is singular, other pronouns which refer to it must also be singular.

RIGHT: Does everyone have <u>his</u> ticket?

WRONG: Does everyone have <u>their</u> ticket?

Other special singular pronouns like <u>everyone</u> are:

SPECIAL SINGULAR PRONOUNS		
everyone	someone	anyone
everybody	somebody	anybody
each	no one	nobody

Exercise 7

Look at the underlined pronoun in each sentence. Draw a circle around the word or words the pronoun stands for. Some of the underlined pronouns are wrong. If they are wrong, write the correct word in the blanks. If the pronoun is correct, write "correct." The first one has been done as an example.

1. Each (person) should sign <u>their</u> name. *his or her*

2. Someone left <u>his</u> wallet on the seat. _____

3. If anyone knows anything, <u>they</u> should call the police. _____

4. Everybody has <u>their</u> own problems. _____

5. The management requests that no one put <u>his</u> feet on the chairs. _____

6. Each girl was asked to select a number and return to <u>their</u> seat. _____

7. Someone called you and said <u>they</u> would call back. _____

8. Everyone who smokes is asked to put out <u>their</u> cigarette. _____

Check your answers before going on.

9. Nobody knows what will happen to <u>them</u> tomorrow. _____

10. To each <u>his</u> own.   _____

11. No one could agree because each had <u>her</u> own idea.   _____

12. Everyone should bring <u>their</u> husband.   _____

13. Every car had <u>its</u> lights on.   _____

14. The police didn't let anyone call <u>their</u> lawyer.   _____

15. Give everyone <u>their</u> presents.   _____

Answers start on page 160.

PRONOUNS AFTER <u>AS</u> AND <u>THAN</u>

Which of the following sentences is correct?

I know Roger better than <u>she</u>.

I know Roger better than <u>her</u>.

Give up? Both are correct. Each means something different, however. The first sentence means:

I know Roger better than <u>she</u> <u>knows</u> <u>Roger</u>.

The second sentence means:

I know Roger better than <u>I</u> <u>know</u> <u>her</u>.

To make sentences shorter and to give them more punch, writers often leave words out. Words have been left out of these two sentences. The educated reader will understand them anyway because one sentence uses a subject pronoun—she—and the other uses an object pronoun—her. Since <u>she</u> is a subject pronoun, it must mean <u>she</u> <u>knows</u>. Since <u>her</u> is an object pronoun, it must mean <u>I</u> <u>know</u> <u>her</u>.

As you can see, once you know grammar well you can pack a lot of meaning into very few words. This is a sign of good writing.

Exercise 8

Write out the full forms of the following sentences. The first two have been done as examples.

1. I trust Sam as much as <u>her</u>.
   I trust Sam as much as I trust her.

2. She dances as well as <u>I</u>.
   She dances as well as I dance.

3. You know Karen better than <u>him</u>.

4. They hate her as much as <u>he</u>.

5. Can she really believe Bonnie more than <u>me</u>?

6. Judy is even more stupid than <u>they</u>.

7. I remember Boris better than <u>her</u>.

8. She believes the newspaper more than <u>I</u>.

Check your answers before going on.

9. You need me more than <u>him</u>.

10. He insulted you more than <u>me</u>.

11. We found Barbara before <u>they</u>.

12.   The salesman called on Toni right after <u>I</u>.

_____

13.   She was laughing at them more than <u>us</u>.

_____

14.   We've known her longer than <u>he</u>.

_____

15.   Susan likes her husband's parents better than <u>he</u>.

_____

Answers start on page 161.

REFLEXIVE PRONOUNS

There is a last set of pronouns which ends with <u>self</u> and <u>selves</u>. They are used mainly when someone does something to himself which could also be done to someone else. They are also used to add force to another pronoun.

> She washed the baby. Then she washed herself.
> Can you lift that by yourself?

The self-pronouns should not be used when subject or object pronouns will do the job.

WRONG: He said his friends would visit his wife and <u>himself</u> next week.

RIGHT: He said his friends would visit his wife and <u>him</u> next week.

Table of Reflexive Pronouns	
myself	ourselves
yourself	yourselves
himself	
herself	themselves
itself	
oneself	

Note that there are no words <u>hisself</u> or <u>theirselves</u>. The correct words are <u>himself</u> and <u>themselves</u>.

Exercise 9

Use words from the Table of Reflexive Pronouns. Write the correct pronouns in the blanks.

1. Leave me alone. I'd rather do it _____.

2. He committed suicide by shooting _____ in the head.

3. She's so selfish, she thinks of no one but _____.

4. Broken machines need spare parts, but the body fixes _____.

5. Her parents died when she and her sisters were young, so they had to take care of _____.

6. Everyone has to be able to take care of _____ in prison.

7. Everyone I knew was busy, so I went by _____ .

8. The members of the city council just voted _____ another raise.

9. My neighbors are very satisfied with _____ .

10. I won't tell you what I think because you should make this decision by _____ .

11. That old man is always talking to _____ .

12. I don't like to leave the children by _____ for too long.

13. This machine is set to shut _____ off.

14. You cannot see _____ as others see you.

15. I gave you as many as I gave _____ .

Answers start on page 161.

REVIEW EXERCISE—PRONOUNS

These exercises will show how much you learned about pronouns. Something is wrong with each sentence. Rewrite each sentence on the line below it so that it is correct.

1. We saw Aunt Jane and himself last Monday morning.

_____

_____

2. Harry never saw his grandson, because he was born after he died.

_____

_____

3. Peter and her both love Chinese food.

_____

4. Who asked you to give it to Mary and he?

_____

5. The man introduced hisself to us and said his name was Sam.

_____

_____

6. When he hit the thief, Ben broke his jaw but cut his hand.

_____

_____

7. The chair fell over on it's back.

_____

8. When the fire alarm rang, everyone left their seat.

_____

_____

9. Between themselves and the police was little respect.

_____

_____

10. No one knows but theyselves.

_____

11.   The new neighbors stick to theirselves.

_____

12.   My father and him have known each other for years.

_____

_____

13.   Is this your's?

_____

14.   The play was a flop because no one knew their lines.

_____

_____

15.   Larry and me are going fishing.

_____

ANSWERS AND EXPLANATIONS—PRONOUNS

Exercise 1

1. Jack
2. My cousins
3. Ellen
4. Bob and Betty
5. The government
6. Carol
7. Kelly's brother
8. Bob's nephew
9. Nancy
10. the letter
11. Nel
12. the flu
13. Phil
14. Evil
15. Drusilla

Exercise 2

There may be other ways to write the sentences clearly. Here are examples.

1. Steve was in the shower when his friend knocked on the door.
2. Craig was only seven years old when his father remarried.
3. The man said his name was Paul and shook Hank's hand.
4. Mrs. Peabody was dead by the time her daughter was married.
5. William's father died just before William was born.

Exercise 3

1. He
2. us
3. them
4. us
5. her
6. We, they
7. them
8. I
9. he
10. her
11. they
12. her
13. them
14. him
15. She

Exercise 4

1.	I	6.	them
2.	her	7.	I
3.	he	8.	me
4.	them	9.	him
5.	he	10.	us

Exercise 5

1.	him	5.	them	9.	correct	13.	correct
2.	us	6.	her	10.	me	14.	him
3.	him	7.	correct	11.	correct	15.	me
4.	me	8.	them	12.	me		

Exercise 6

1.	its	5.	your	9.	ours	13.	hers
2.	theirs	6.	theirs	10.	mine	14.	its
3.	ours	7.	It's	11.	your	15.	they're
4.	My	8.	their	12.	their		

Exercise 7

1. Person; his or her
2. Someone; his is correct
3. anyone; he or she
4. Everybody; his or her
5. no one; his is correct
6. girl; her
7. Someone; he or she
8. Everyone; his or her
9. Nobody; him or her
10. each; his is correct
11. each; her is correct
12. Everyone; her
13. car; its is correct
14. anyone; his or her
15. everyone; his or her

Exercise 8

Some of your sentences may be slightly different.

1. I trust Sam as much as I trust her.
2. She dances as well as I dance.
3. You know Karen better than you know him.
4. They hate her as much as he hates her.
5. Can she really believe Bonnie more than she believes me?
6. Judy is even more stupid than they are.
7. I remember Boris better than I remember her.
8. She believes the newspaper more than I believe the newspaper.
9. You need me more than you need him.
10. He insulted you more than he insulted me.
11. We found Barbara before they found Barbara.
12. The salesman called on Toni right after I called on Toni.
13. She was laughing at them more than she was laughing at us.
14. We've known her longer than he has known her.
15. Susan likes her husband's parents better than he likes her husband's parents.

Exercise 9

1. myself
2. himself
3. herself
4. itself
5. themselves
6. himself or herself
7. myself
8. themselves
9. themselves
10. yourself
11. himself
12. themselves
13. itself
14. yourself
15. myself

ANSWERS AND EXPLANATIONS—REVIEW EXERCISE

Some of your answers might be slightly different. Double check these with a friend.

1. We saw Aunt Jane and him last Monday morning.
2. Because Harry died before his grandson was born, Harry never saw him.
3. Peter and she both love Chinese food.
4. Who asked you to give it to Mary and him?
5. The man introduced himself to us and said his name was Sam.
6. Ben broke the thief's jaw when he hit him but cut his own hand.
7. The chair fell over on its back.
8. When the fire alarm rang, everyone left his (or her) seat.
9. Between them and the police was little respect.
10. No one knows but himself (or herself).
11. The new neighbors stick to themselves.
12. My father and he have known each other for years.
13. Is this yours?
14. The play was a flop because no one knew his (or her) lines.
15. Larry and I are going fishing.

6 | ADJECTIVES AND ADVERBS

ADJECTIVES

Adjectives are words that change the meaning of nouns. For example, here are three adjectives that change the noun man:

fat man
thin man
tall man

Fat, thin, and tall are adjectives.

Exercise 1

Fill in the blanks in the following story. Any words that fit are adjectives.

It was a _____ day. Martha felt _____ even before she got out of bed. Her breakfast coffee was _____, her toast was _____, and her eggs were _____. Work was even more _____ than usual. Her boss was really _____ to her. After work she went shopping at the _____ store across the street. She bought _____ shoes and a _____ dress. This made her feel _____.

Answers start on page 176.

-ER

Most adjectives have an -er form:

Adjective	-Er Form
tall	taller
quick	quicker
heavy	heavier

As you can see, you just add -er to most adjectives.

A few adjectives, however, are irregular:

some	more (not somer)
bad	worse (not badder)
good	better (not gooder)

Long adjectives sound funny if you add -er to them. If you think an adjective sounds funny with -er, you can put more in front of it instead. Using more is the same as adding -er.

more careful	(instead of carefuller)
more useful	(instead of usefuller)
more likely	(instead of likelier)

It is often up to you whether to use more or -er with an adjective. For instance, likelier and more likely are both correct.

These -er and more adjectives are often used with the word than.

Exercise 2

Fill in the blanks in the following sentences with -er and more adjectives.

1. Children are *smaller, more honest,* and *younger* than adults.

2. Women are _taller_, _more_, and _____ than men.

3. Men are _taller_, _more_, and _____ than women.

4. Love is _likelier_, _more_, and _____ than hate.

5. Paper is _heavier_, _____, and _____ than wood.

6. Oatmeal is _more_, _better_, and _____ than potato chips.

7. Milk is _more_, _better_, and _____ than water.

8. An apple is _more_, _____, and _____ than a walnut.

9. A coat is _heavier_, _more_, and _____ than a dress.

10. Dogs are _____, _____, and _____ than people.

11. Zippers are _____, _____, and _____ than buttons.

Answers start on page 176.

EST

The -er form is used when comparing one thing to another:

Children are smaller than adults.

But when you want to single out one thing in a group, you need the -est form:

> Steve was the smallest child in the class.

Most adjectives just add -est:

tall	tallest
quick	quickest
heavy	heaviest

Some are irregular:

some	most (not sommest)
bad	worst (not baddest)
good	best (not goodest)

Using <u>most</u> is the same as adding -est:

most careful	(instead of carefullest)
most useful	(instead of usefullest)
most likely	(instead of likeliest)

Exercise 3

Each sentence has two blanks. Put the plain form of any adjective in the first blank. Put the -est or <u>most</u> form of the same adjective in the second blank.

1. John is _silly_, but Henry is the _silliest_.

2. Cats are _bad_, but dogs are the _worst_.

3. I am _tallest_, but you are the _heaviest_ of the whole group.

4. Sally is _good_, but Jim is the _goodest_.

5. Beer is _quick_, but vodka is the _quickest_.

6. Rock and roll is _____ but opera is the _____.

7. Getting old is _____, but dying is the _____.

8. English class is _____, but math class is the _____.

9. Having to wait is _____, but getting refused is the _____.

10. Receiving a gift is _____, but giving is the _____.

11. Walking is _____, but running is the _____.

12. Trying is _____, but succeeding is the _____.

Answers start on page 177.

THIS, THESE, THAT, AND THOSE

This, these, that, and those are adjectives. This and these are over **here;** that and those are over **there.** This and that are singular; these and those are plural.

> this chair (one chair, over here)
> these chairs (many chairs, over here)
> that chair (one chair, over there)
> those chairs (many chairs, over there)

People sometimes use the word them in place of this, that, these, and those:

> How do you like them apples?

This use of the word them is a sign of a poor education. Use:

> these apples
>
> those apples
>
> but not: them apples

Exercise 4

Cross out them where it is incorrectly used as an adjective. Write "these" or "those" in the blank. Where them is correctly used—as a pronoun—draw a circle around it and write "correct" in the blank.

1. I like ~~them~~.   *correct*
2. I dislike ~~them~~ kinds of people.   *those*
3. In ~~them~~ days, beer was five cents a glass.   *those*
4. We know them from when we lived in Montana.
5. You should get one of ~~them~~ flyswatters.   *those*
6. ~~Them~~ cars don't have enough power.   *these*
7. We saw them on Montague Street.

Check your answers before going on.

8. We bought them a present.
9. We gave them old clothes away to the Salvation Army.
10. ~~Them~~ things don't last long.   *these*
11. She told them everything they wanted to hear.
12. ~~Them~~ questions are too hard.   *those*

Check your answers before going on.

13. He learned about it from them.   *those*
14. Them boxes have got to go.   *these*
15. It was between Susan and them.
16. We wished them a very merry Christmas.
17. You can't trust them politicians.

Answers start on page 177.

DOUBLE NEGATIVES

It's considered bad writing to use two negative words

where one will do. What's a negative word? A negative word is a word in the <u>no</u> and <u>not</u> family. For instance:

no	never
not	nothing
hardly	scarcely
none	no one
nobody	don't

You shouldn't use more than one of these words unless you have to. For instance:

I don't know nothing about it.

This sentence has too many negative words. Either take out <u>don't</u>, or change <u>nothing</u>:

I know nothing about it.
I don't know anything about it.

Exercise 5

Each of these sentences has too many negative words. Rewrite the sentences.

1. He doesn't hardly never come.
    He hardly ever comes. or: *He almost never comes.*

2. She never says nothing.
    She never says anything.

3. We couldn't see nothing.

4. Fish don't have no feet.

5.   That doesn't have nothing to do with it.

_____

6.   Don't never talk to me that way.

_____

7.   There wasn't scarcely no water there.

_____

8.   There isn't nobody in this town who dances like you.

_____

9.   We haven't seen none of them.

_____

10.   I haven't never had such a good time.

_____

11.   We haven't never heard of no animal like that.

_____

12.   Don't never let a woman know how much you like her.

_____

13.   Nobody doesn't know nothing.

_____

Answers start on page 178.

ADVERBS

Adverbs are words that change the meaning of verbs. For example, here are three adverbs that change the verb runs:

He runs <u>slowly</u>.   He runs <u>quickly</u>.   He runs <u>gracefully</u>.

Notice that these three adverbs end with -<u>ly</u>. <u>Ly</u> is a common ending for adverbs.

Exercise 6

Fill in the blanks with adverbs that end with <u>ly</u>. Underline the verbs that the adverbs change.

1. The audience <u>applauded</u>   *loudly*   .

2. The phone <u>rang</u> again   *immediately* .

3. The police entered _____.

4. Nancy kissed Peter _____.

5. After four drinks, Sam drove _____.

6. The boy approached his father _____.

7. The electric heater started _____.

8. The cat licked its fur _____.

9. A well-tuned engine runs _____.

10. Pamela waited at the corner _____.

11. The radio played _____.

12. They thanked their host _____.

13. Boris' teeth chattered _____.

14. Broken bones heal _____.

15. The wind roared _____.

Answers start on page 178.

ADJECTIVE OR ADVERB?

Which of these sentences is correct?
The boy walked <u>slow</u>. The boy walked <u>slowly</u>.

The second sentence is correct. The word <u>slowly</u> changes <u>walk</u>. It tells how the boy walked. <u>Walked</u> is a verb. Verbs are changed by adverbs. <u>Slowly</u> is an adverb, but <u>slow</u> is an adjective. The adjective <u>slow</u> would be correct in a sentence where it changed a noun. For instance, <u>slow</u> is correct in this sentence, where it changes the noun <u>boy</u>:

The boy was slow.

Exercise 7

Choose the correct word and write it on the line. Underline the noun or verb that it changes.

1. Cynthia <u>spoke</u> (serious, seriously).   *seriously*

2. <u>Malcolm</u> is (honest, honestly).   *honest*

3. The door opened (sudden, suddenly).   _____

4. The nurses treated him (rough, roughly).   _____

5. The light was too (bright, brightly).   _____

6. The pot fell (heavy, heavily) on the floor.   _____

7. The terrier snarled (menacing, menacingly).   _____

8. She wrote us a (sad, sadly) letter.   _____

Check your answers before going on.

9. We watched the fire (close, closely).   _____

10. The old man emitted (harsh, harshly) _____ coughs.

11. This pen writes very (smooth, smoothly).   _____

12. He made a (generous, generously) dona- _____ tion.

13. They made a (cautious, cautiously) deci-   _____
     sion.

14. Tom (meek, meekly) agreed.   _____

15. The child answered (polite, politely).   _____

Answers start on page 179.

REVIEW EXERCISE—ADJECTIVES AND ADVERBS

These exercises will show what you know about adjectives and adverbs. The word underlined in each sentence may be wrong. Check (✔) the correct form of the word. If the sentence is correct, check (5) no change.

1. Mark is <u>oldest</u> than Judy.

    _____(1) older

    _____(2) more old

    _____(3) most old

    _____(4) olderest

    _____(5) no change

2. <u>Them</u> days are gone forever.

    _____(1) That

    _____(2) This

    _____(3) These

    _____(4) Those

    _____(5) no change

3. <u>I don't have nothing to do with it.</u>

    _____(1) I ain't got nothing to do with it.

    _____(2) I don't hardly have nothing to do with it.

    _____(3) I have nothing to do with it.

    _____(4) I don't haven't nothing to do with it.

    _____(5) no change

4. This is the <u>most</u> <u>happiest</u> day of my life.

_____(1)   more happiest

_____(2)   most happier

_____(3)   happiest

_____(4)   happierest

_____(5)   no change

5. He smiled <u>coldly</u> at her tears.

_____(1)   cold

_____(2)   with cold

_____(3)   coldily

_____(4)   colder

_____(5)   no change

6. The dog crept <u>slowly</u> to the table.

_____(1)   slow

_____(2)   with slowness

_____(3)   slovenly

_____(4)   slower

_____(5)   no change

7. Greta frightened <u>them</u> pigeons.

_____(1)   this

_____(2)   that

_____(3)   those

_____(4)   any

_____(5)   no change

8. The murder was the <u>horriblest</u> that ever occurred here.

_____(1)   horribler

_____(2)   most horrible

_____(3)   more horrible

_____(4)   horribly

_____(5)   no change

9. Karen dresses <u>more carefully</u> since her husband died.

_____(1)   carefuller

_____(2)   more careful

_____(3)   carefullier

_____(4)   very careful

_____(5)   no change

10. The plumber gave <u>them</u> some good advice.

_____(1)   this

_____(2)   that

_____(3)   those

_____(4)   these

_____(5)   no change

ANSWERS AND EXPLANATIONS—ADJECTIVES AND ADVERBS

Exercise 1

The words you used might have been different. Any word that fits is an adjective.

It was a <u>splendid</u> day. Martha felt <u>fine</u> even before she got out of bed. Her breakfast coffee was <u>fragrant</u>, her toast was <u>warm</u>, and her eggs were <u>perfect</u>. Work was even more <u>fun</u> than usual. Her boss was really <u>nice</u> to her. After work she went shopping at the <u>department</u> store across the street. She bought <u>dress</u> shoes and a <u>party</u> dress. This made her feel <u>elegant</u>.

Exercise 2

Your words might be different. These are given only as examples.

1. smaller, more honest, and younger
2. kinder, smarter, and more generous
3. kinder, smarter, and more generous
4. healthier, more productive, and more complicated
5. softer, whiter, and more flexible
6. blander, lumpier, and more nutritious
7. creamier, tastier, and more expensive
8. redder, sweeter, and larger
9. warmer, longer, and more expensive
10. shorter, friendlier, and more loyal
11. easier, noisier, and more efficient

Exercise 3

Your words might be different. These are given only as examples.

1. silly, silliest
2. bad, worst
3. boring, most boring
4. young, youngest
5. costly, most costly
6. popular, most popular
7. scary, scariest
8. crowded, most crowded
9. frustrating, most frustrating
10. nice, nicest
11. fast, fastest
12. sweet, sweetest

Exercise 4

1. correct
2. those
3. those days
4. correct
5. those flyswatters or these flyswatters
6. Those cars or These cars
7. correct
8. correct
9. these old clothes or those old clothes
10. Those things or These things
11. correct
12. Those questions or These questions
13. correct
14. Those boxes or These boxes
15. correct
16. correct
17. those politicians or these politicians

Exercise 5

1. He hardly ever comes. or He almost never comes.
2. She never says anything.
3. We could see nothing. or We couldn't see anything.
4. Fish don't have feet. or Fish have no feet.
5. That doesn't have anything to do with it. or That has nothing to do with it.
6. Don't ever talk to me that way. or Never talk to me that way.
7. There was scarcely any water there.
8. There isn't anybody in this town who dances like you. or Nobody in this town dances like you.
9. We haven't seen any of them. or We have seen none of them.
10. I haven't ever had such a good time. or I never had such a good time.
11. We haven't ever heard of an animal like that. or We never heard of an animal like that.
12. Don't ever let a woman know how much you like her. or Never let a woman know how much you like her.
13. Nobody knows anything.

Exercise 6

Your adverbs may be different. These are given as examples only.

1. applauded loudly
2. rang immediately
3. entered suddenly
4. kissed tenderly
5. drove badly
6. approached timidly
7. started quickly
8. licked slowly
9. runs smoothly
10. waited patiently
11. played loudly
12. thanked politely
13. chattered loudly
14. heal slowly
15. roared fiercely

Exercise 7

1. Cynthia spoke seriously.
2. Malcolm is honest.
3. The door opened suddenly.
4. The nurses treated him roughly.
5. The light was too bright.
6. The pot fell heavily on the floor.
7. The terrier snarled menacingly.
8. She wrote us a sad letter.
9. We watched the fire closely.
10. The old man emitted harsh coughs.
11. This pen writes very smoothly.
12. He made a generous donation.
13. They made a cautious decision.
14. Tom meekly agreed.
15. The child answered politely.

ANSWERS AND EXPLANATIONS—REVIEW EXERCISE

1. (1) older
2. (4) Those
3. (3) I have nothing to do with it.
4. (3) happiest
5. (5) no change
6. (5) no change
7. (3) those
8. (2) most horrible
9. (5) no change
10. (5) no change

POST-TEST

Directions: The Post-Test gives a final test of the skills you have built. Like the Pre-Test, the 30 questions here test your writing skills in the areas that were covered in this book.

Your skills in these areas should be stronger than they were when you started *Building Basic Skills in Writing, Book 1.*

Follow the directions for each part. There is no time limit, so you may take as long as you need for each question. When you finish, check your answers. Answers and Explanations start at the end of the Post-Test. Fill in the rest of the Test Score Record that you started after the Pre-Test.

1 SENTENCES

Four groups of words tell a short story in each of the following. Read each group of words and look at the punctuation mark at the end. One of these marks may be wrong. If so, put a check mark (✔)next to the number of the group of words whose punctuation is wrong. Check number (5) if there is no error.

1. _____(1)   As he came around the turn, Phil stepped on the brakes.
   _____(2)   What was wrong?
   _____(3)   Oh, no.
   _____(4)   The brakes had failed.
   _____(5)   no error

2. _____(1)   The phone rang at 8:00 in the evening.
   _____(2)   It was his daughter Ellen.

_____(3) She asked if he was feeling better?

_____(4) Tears came into his eyes.

_____(5) no error

3. _____(1) Everyone at work knew that Chuck was on the wagon.

_____(2) They kept giving him cans of juice.

_____(3) If they filled him up with juice

_____(4) he couldn't drink beer.

_____(5) no error

4. _____(1) Maria was training for the marathon.

_____(2) She ran 12 miles a day.

_____(3) seven days a week.

_____(4) She wanted to win.

_____(5) no error

5. _____(1) Will I accept your offer?

_____(2) Never!

_____(3) Under no circumstances!

_____(4) Absolutely not!

_____(5) no error

2 NOUNS

Four words have been underlined in each sentence. If the underlined word is wrong, put a check mark (✔) in front of its number. If there is no error, check number 5.

6. Historians believe that king Charles made a mistake.

_____(1) king

_____(2) Charles

_____(3)   made
_____(4)   mistake
_____(5)   no error

7.   The world's tallest Mountains are the Himalayas.
_____(1)   world's
_____(2)   tallest
_____(3)   Mountains
_____(4)   Himalayas
_____(5)   no error

8.   Girl's coats are upstairs; women's shoes are downstairs.
_____(1)   Girl's
_____(2)   coats
_____(3)   women's
_____(4)   shoes
_____(5)   no error

9.   Russ's wife's aunt borrowed Lisa's book's.
_____(1)   Russ's
_____(2)   wife's
_____(3)   Lisa's
_____(4)   book's
_____(5)   no error

10.   The magazine published pictures of babie's faces.
_____(1)   The
_____(2)   magazine
_____(3)   babie's
_____(4)   faces
_____(5)   no error

3 VERBS

Four words have been underlined in each sentence. If the underlined word is wrong, put a check mark (✔) next to its number. If there is no error, check number (5).

11. She <u>like</u> to <u>talk</u>, but you <u>don't</u> have to <u>listen</u>.

_____(1)   like

_____(2)   talk

_____(3)   don't

_____(4)   listen

_____(5)   no error

12. He <u>is</u> one <u>of</u> the people who <u>plays</u> in the band with <u>me</u>.

_____(1)   is

_____(2)   of

_____(3)   plays

_____(4)   me

_____(5)   no error

13. <u>Does</u> your dog and cat always <u>get</u> along so <u>well</u>?

_____(1)   Does

_____(2)   your

_____(3)   get

_____(4)   well

_____(5)   no error

14. There <u>is</u> still a few <u>more</u> bills to <u>pay</u> <u>this</u> month.

_____(1)   is

_____(2)   more

_____(3)   pay

_____(4)   this

_____(5)   no error

15.   I am sure she has no idea what you meant to say.

_____(1)   am
_____(2)   has
_____(3)   meant
_____(4)   say
_____(5)   no error

4 MORE ABOUT VERBS

Four words have been underlined in each sentence. If the underlined word is wrong, put a check mark (✔) next to its number. If there is no error, check number 5.

16.   My husband done bought it without telling me.

_____(1)   done
_____(2)   bought
_____(3)   telling
_____(4)   me
_____(5)   no error

17.   They told me that Gary don't come around here too often.

_____(1)   told
_____(2)   that
_____(3)   don't
_____(4)   come
_____(5)   no error

18.   I think we sung that song already, but we can do it again.

_____(1)   think
_____(2)   sung
_____(3)   can
_____(4)   do
_____(5)   no error

19. I <u>don't</u> <u>trust</u> you this time, because <u>you</u> have <u>forgot</u> too
    many times before.
    _____(1)   don't
    _____(2)   trust
    _____(3)   you
    _____(4)   forgot
    _____(5)   no error

20. I <u>can't</u> <u>hear</u> what <u>you're</u> <u>saying</u>.
    _____(1)   can't
    _____(2)   hear
    _____(3)   you're
    _____(4)   saying
    _____(5)   no error

5 PRONOUNS

Four words have been underlined in each sentence. If
the underlined word is wrong, put a check mark (✔) next to
its number. If there is no error, check number 5.

21. The argument <u>between</u> Doris and <u>she</u> <u>is</u> <u>over</u>.
    _____(1)   between
    _____(2)   she
    _____(3)   is
    _____(4)   over
    _____(5)   no error

22. <u>Did</u> <u>they</u> give <u>it</u> to Paul and <u>him</u>?
    _____(1)   Did
    _____(2)   they
    _____(3)   it
    _____(4)   him
    _____(5)   no error

23. Mr. Jones and <u>her</u> should <u>think</u> <u>more</u> about <u>it</u>.
_____(1)   her
_____(2)   think
_____(3)   more
_____(4)   it
_____(5)   no error

24. It seems to <u>me</u> that <u>your</u> car needs to have <u>it's</u> alignment checked.
_____(1)   It
_____(2)   me
_____(3)   your
_____(4)   it's
_____(5)   no error

25. Rembrandt painted <u>this</u> portrait of <u>hisself</u> and hung <u>it</u> in <u>his</u> studio.
_____(1)   this
_____(2)   hisself
_____(3)   it
_____(4)   his
_____(5)   no error

6 ADJECTIVES AND ADVERBS

Four words have been underlined in each sentence. If the underlined word is wrong, put a check mark (✔) next to the number. If there is no error, check number 5.

26. He has <u>got</u> to <u>be</u> the <u>most</u> stupidest man I <u>know</u>.
_____(1)   got
_____(2)   be
_____(3)   most
_____(4)   know
_____(5)   no error

27. <u>Them</u> kind of apples <u>is</u> only good <u>for</u> <u>baking</u>.

      (1)   Them

      (2)   is

      (3)   for

      (4)   baking

      (5)   no error

28. Don't <u>never</u> suggest <u>such</u> a thing <u>to</u> <u>me</u> again.

      (1)   never

      (2)   such

      (3)   to

      (4)   me

      (5)   no error

29. He <u>drives</u> <u>more</u> <u>careful</u> <u>since</u> his accident.

      (1)   drives

      (2)   more

      (3)   careful

      (4)   since

      (5)   no error

30. I <u>don't</u> like to argue with <u>him</u>, because he takes <u>every-thing</u> so <u>seriously</u>.

      (1)   don't

      (2)   him

      (3)   everything

      (4)   seriously

      (5)   no error

ANSWERS AND EXPLANATIONS—POST-TEST

1 *Sentences*

1. (3) This sentence should end with an exclamation mark.
2. (3) This sentence should end with a period.
3. (5) no error
4. (2) There should be no period here. This is not the end of the sentence.
5. (5) no error

2 *Nouns*

6. (1) king should be King.
7. (3) Mountains should be mountains.
8. (1) Girl's should be Girls'.
9. (4) book's should be books.
10. (3) babie's should be babies'.

3 *Verbs*

11. (1) like should be likes.
12. (3) plays should be play.
13. (1) Does should be Do.
14. (1) is should be are.
15. (5) no error

4 *More About Verbs*

16. (1) done is not needed in this sentence.
17. (3) don't should be doesn't.
18. (2) sung should be sang.
19. (4) forgot should be forgotten.
20. (5) no error

5 *Pronouns*

21. (2) she should be her.
22. (5) no error

23. (1) <u>her</u> should be <u>she</u>.

24. (4) <u>it's</u> should be <u>its</u>.

25. (2) <u>hisself</u> should be <u>himself</u>.

6 *Adjectives and Adverbs*

26. (3) <u>most</u> is not needed when <u>stupidest</u> is used.

27. (1) <u>Them</u> should be <u>This</u> or <u>That</u>.

28. (1) <u>never</u> is not needed in this sentence; <u>ever</u> could be used instead.

29. (3) <u>careful</u> should be <u>carefully</u>.

30. (5) no error

ANswer and explanation is adjectives and adverbs.
The words you used might have been different.
Any word that fit is an [adjective.]
   It was a splendid day. martha felt even
before she got out of bed. Her breakfast coffe
was faagrant, her toast was worm, and her
eggs were Perfect. Work was even more fun
than usual. Her boss was really nice to her
After work she went shopping at the department
store across the street. She bought dress
shoes and a Party dress. This made her feel
elegant.

Steve was in the shower when his friend knocked on the door.

Craig was only seven years old when his father remarried.

The man said his name was Paul and shook hank's hand.

MR. Peabody was dead by the time her daughter was married.

William's father died just before William was born.

Exercise 1.

Answer and explanation's adjective's = and adverbs

The words you used might have been different. any word that fit is an adjective.

IT was a splendid day. martha felt even before she got out of bed. Her breakfast caffe was fragrant her toast was warm

and her eggs were perfect. work was even more fun than usual. Her. After work she went shopping at the department store across the street she bought dress shoes and a party